Where Wear to 2004

THE INSIDER'S GUIDE TO SAN FRANCISCO SHOPPING

Fairchild & Gallagher

NEW YORK • LONDON

PUBLISHERS
Jill Fairchild & Gerri Gallagher

WRITER
Beth LaDove

COPY EDITOR
John Graham

PREVIOUS WRITERS
Heidi Lender, Erika Lenkert

DESIGN / PRODUCTION ARTIST
Jeff Baker

COVER DESIGN
Richard Chapman

CARTOGRAPHER
Candida Kennedy

DISTRIBUTION, SALES AND MARKETING
The Julie Craik Consultancy

Where to Wear, San Francisco, 2004 Edition
ISBN 0-9720215-4-X

666 Fifth Avenue
PMB 377
New York, NY 10103
TEL 212-969-0138
TOLL-FREE 1-877-714-SHOP (7467)
FAX 212-315-1534
E-MAIL wheretowear@aol.com

10 Cinnamon Row, Plantation Wharf, London SW11 3TW
TEL 020 7801 1381
E-MAIL wheretowear@onetel.net.uk

www.wheretowear.com

Table of Contents

Introduction

Dear San Francisco Shopper,

Welcome to *Where to Wear*, the world's most detailed and authoritative directory of clothing and accessory stores. *Where to Wear* annually updates its collection of global guides, making your travels through the world's fashion cities a breeze. We pioneered in 1999 with *Where to Wear New York*, and we have since added London, Paris, Los Angeles, San Francisco and Italy, which includes Florence, Milan and Rome.

The 2004 edition of *Where to Wear San Francisco* has all the information you'll need to look and feel great. We describe over 400 different clothing and accessories stores, ranging from the global celebrity names of Union Square and Fillmore to out-of-the-way treasure-houses. *Where to Wear* shows visitors where to begin and San Franciscans where to go next. If you want the best vintage value or the bonniest baby boutique, you'll find them using *Where to Wear*.

These are the only shopping guides written by a team of top fashion journalists. We have our fingers on the pulse of the ever-changing fashion world. We've tromped through each and every store to discover what's fabulous, functional, frumpy, fancy or frightful in them this season. We tell you what the store and its merchandise are all about and who its target customer is, and we list the address, phone number and opening hours. We've marked those stores that merit special consideration with a star (☆), and occasionally we have something sweet (or not so sweet) to say about the staff's helpfulness or attitude. Please let us know if you disagree.

And to make your life even simpler we have included ten pages of user-friendly maps and two separate indexes grouping the stores both by category and by location. Shopping has never been easier! In addition, you'll find the best addresses for beauty treatments, fitness studios, day spas, couture dry cleaners, shoe repair shops, specialty stores (for beads, ribbons, etc) and much else.

Life is not all shopping, of course, so you will also find a list of in-store restaurants and other delightful lunch spots. It's an eclectic list, chosen by our experts for your fun and convenience.

So rev up your credit card and get going, and make sure to keep *W2W* in your handbag, briefcase or backpack.

—Jill Fairchild & Gerri Gallagher

Jill Fairchild Melhado, daughter of fashion world legend and *W* magazine founder John Fairchild, worked as an intern at *Glamour* magazine, *GQ* and *Vogue*. Ms Fairchild has also worked for Ailes Communications, a television production company, and in the late Eighties she founded and ran her own accessories company.

Gerri Gallagher is a Condé Nast editor who has lived in Europe for 15 years. She was the managing editor of Fairchild Publication's *W Europe* from 1990 to 1993 and is currently associate editor of *Tatler* magazine in London.

Julie Craik, *Where to Wear* partner and director of sales, marketing and distribution has worked in publishing for 20 years. Before joining *W2W* she was associate publisher of *Tatler* magazine and had previously worked for the National Magazine Company.

Where to Wear 2004

Best Picks

A Girl and her Dog
Ab Fits
Abigail Morgan
Alençon Couture Bridal

Alla Prima
American Rag Cie
The Bar
Baxter Hull

Behind the Post Office
Blu
Brown Eyed Girl
Cielo

Cool World Sports
Dantone
Diesel
Dish

dress
emily lee
Erica Tanov
Fetish

Gimme Shoes
The Grocery Store
Harputs
Heather

Heidi Says
Jeremys
Joe Pye
Kate Spade

Kati Koós
Knitz & Leather
Marc Jacobs
Margaret O'Leary

Metier
Mudpie
Nida
Nomads

Oceana Rain
Ooma
Riley James
Rolo SoMa

Smith Williams
Subterranean Shoe Room
Sugar Poppy
Susan

Velvet da Vinci
Ver Unica
Waterlilies
Workshop

In-Store Restaurants

Armani Café at Emporio Armani   415-677-9010
1 Grant Avenue

Briazz at Birkenstock   415-392-1750
79 O'Farrell Street

The Rotunda at Neiman Marcus   415-362-4777
150 Stockton Street

The Cheesecake Factory at Macy's   415-391-4444
251 Geary Street

City Center Grill at Nordstrom   415-977-5155
San Francisco Shopping Centre
865 Market Street

Restaurants

The following is a select list of restaurants perfect for
lunching during your shopping spree.

BERKELEY/OAKLAND

Bette's Oceanview Diner (American)   510-644-3230
1807a 4th Street

Café Fanny (Brunch, Crêpes, Sandwiches)   510-524-5447
1603 San Pablo Avenue

Café Rouge (French Bistro)   510-525-1440
1782 4th Street

O Chamé (Japanese)   510-841-8783
1830 4th Street

Castro Blue (Hip American Diner)   415-863-2583
2337 Market Street

Chow (Italian)   415-552-2469
215 Church Street

Firewood Café (Italian)   415-252-0999
4248 18th Street

Home   415-503-0333
2100 Market Street

La Mediterranée (Middle Eastern)   415-431-7210
288 Noe Street

COW HOLLOW
Betelnut Pejiu Wu (Pan-Asian)   415-929-8855
2030 Union Street

Pane e Vino (Italian)   415-346-2111
3011 Steiner Street

PlumpJack Cafe (Cal-Mediterranean)   415-563-4755
3127 Fillmore Street

Rose's Café (Sandwiches, Soups, Salads)   415-775-2200
2298 Union Street

Via Vai (Italian)   415-441-2111
1715 Union Street

HAIGHT-ASHBURY
Cha Cha Cha (Caribbean Tapas)   415-386-5758
1801 Haight Street

Kate's Kitchen (American)   415-626-3984
471 Haight Street

HAYES VALLEY
Absinthe (French Brasserie)   415-551-1590
398 Hayes Street

Citizen Cake   415-861-2228
(Soups, Sandwiches, Salads, Desserts)
399 Grove Street

Zuni (Italian-Mediterranean)   415-552-2522
1658 Market Street

MARIN

Buckeye Roadhouse (American)　　　　415-331-2600
15 Shoreline Highway　　　　　　　　　　Mill Valley

Joe's Taco Lounge (Mexican)　　　　　415-383-8164
382 Miller Avenue　　　　　　　　　　　Mill Valley

Lark Creek Inn (American)　　　　　　415-924-7766
234 Magnolia Avenue　　　　　　　　　　Larkspur

Sunnyside Café　　　　　　　　　　　415-388-5260
(Breakfast, Sandwiches, Soups)
31 Sunnyside Avenue　　　　　　　　　　Mill Valley

Yankee Pier (New England-style seafood)　415-924-7676
286 Magnolia Avenue

MARINA

Andalé Taqueria (cheap, fresh Mexican)　415-749-0506
2150 Chestnut Street

Café Marimba (Mexican)　　　　　　　415-776-1506
2317 Chestnut Street

Greens (Vegetarian)　　　　　　　　　415-771-6222
Fort Mason Center, Building A

The Grove (Coffeehouse, Sandwiches)　415-474-4843
2250 Chestnut Street

Pluto's (American)　　　　　　　　　　415-775-8867
3258 Scott Street

MISSION

Herbivore (Vegan/Vegetarian)　　　　　415-826-5657
983 Valencia Street

Luna Park (French-Italian)　　　　　　415-553-8584
694 Valencia Street

Ramblas Tapas Bar (Spanish Tapas)　　415-565-0207
557 Valencia Street

Ti Couz (Crêpes)　　　　　　　　　　　415-252-7373
3108 16th Street

NOE VALLEY

Eric's (Chinese)　　　　　　　　　　　415-282-0919
1500 Church Street

Miss Millie's (Brunch, New American)　415-285-5598
4123 24th Street

Pasta Pomodoro (Italian)　　　　　　　415-920-9904
4000 24th Street

NORTH BEACH

The House (Pan-Asian)   **415-986-8612**
1230 Grant Avenue

L'Osteria del Forno (Italian)   **415-982-1124**
519 Columbus Avenue

Mama's on Washington Square   **415-362-6421**
(Brunch, American)
1701 Stockton Street

Mario's Bohemian Cigar Store Café   **415-362-0536**
(Italian)
566 Columbus Avenue

Moose's (Regional American)   **415-989-7800**
1652 Stockton Street

North Beach (Italian)   **415-392-1700**
1512 Stockton Street

Rose Pistola (Italian)   **415-399-0499**
532 Columbus Avenue

PACIFIC HEIGHTS

Florio (French Bistro)   **415-775-4300**
1915 Fillmore Street

Chez Nous (Mediterranean Tapas)   **415-441-8044**
1911 Fillmore Street

La Mediterranée (Middle Eastern)   **415-921-2956**
2210 Fillmore Street

PENINSULA

Lark Creek (All-American, farm-fresh)   **650-344-9444**
50 East 3rd Avenue (Benjamin Franklin Hotel)   San Mateo

Pisces (Seafood)   **650-401-7500**
1190 California Drive   Burlingame

Pluto's (American)   **650-853-1556**
482 University Avenue   Palo Alto

Spago Palo Alto (Californian)   **650-833-1000**
265 Lytton Avenue   Palo Alto

Viognier (Cal/Mediterranean)   **650-685-3727**
222 East 4th Avenue (Draeger's Market)   San Mateo

Zibibbo (Mediterranean)   **650-328-6722**
430 Kipling Street   Palo Alto

PRESIDIO HEIGHTS

Garibaldis on Presidio (Cal/Mediterranean)   **415-563-8841**
347 Presidio Avenue

Ella's Restaurant (Brunch, American)   **415-441-5669**
500 Presidio Avenue

SOMA

Azie (French/Asian)   **415-538-9444**
826 Folsom Street

bacar (American Brasserie)   **415-904-4100**
448 Brannan Street

Caffe Centro (Sandwiches, Salads)   **415-882-1500**
102 South Park Avenue

Fringale (French)   **415-543-0573**
570 4th Street

Hawthorne Lane (Californian)   **415-777-9779**
22 Hawthorne Street

Le Charm (French Bistro)   **415-546-6128**
315 5th Street

Momo's (American)   **415-227-8660**
760 2nd Street

South Park Café (French Bistro)   **415-495-7275**
108 South Park Avenue

Tu Lan (Vietnamese)   **415-626-0927**
8 6th Street

XYZ (California/French)   **415-817-7836**
181 3rd Street (W Hotel)

UNION SQUARE

Aqua (Seafood)   **415-956-9662**
252 California Street

B44 (Spanish)   **415-986-6287**
44 Belden Place

Café Bastille (French Brasserie)   **415-986-5673**
22 Belden Place

Café Claude (French Bistro)   **415-392-3515**
7 Claude Lane

Café de la Presse (French Bistro)   **415-249-0900**
352 Grant Avenue

Campton Place (French)   **415-955-5555**
340 Stockton Street (Campton Place Hotel)

Farallon (Seafood)   **415-956-6969**
450 Post Street

Fifth Floor (New French)   **415-348-1555**
12 4th Street (Hotel Palomar)

Grand Café (French Bistro)   415-292-0101
501 Geary Street

Kuleto's (Italian)   415-397-7720
221 Powell Street (Villa Florence Hotel)

Metropol   415-732-7777
(Italian café with panini, salads)
168 Sutter Street

Ponzu (Pan-Asian)   415-775-7979
401 Taylor Street

Sanraku (Japanese & Sushi)   415-771-0803
704 Sutter Street

Scala's Bistro (French/Italian)   415-395-8555
432 Powell Street (Sir Francis Drake Hotel)

Clothing & Shoe Size Equivalents

Children's Clothing

American	3	4	5	6	6X
Continental	98	104	110	116	122
British	18	20	22	24	26

Children's Shoes

American	8	9	10	11	12	12	1	2	3
Continental	24	25	27	28	29	30	32	33	34
British	7	8	9	10	11	12	13	1	2

Ladies' Coats, Dresses, Skirts

American	3	5	7	9	11	12	13	14	15
Continental	36	38	38	40	40	42	42	44	44
British	8	10	11	12	13	14	15	16	17

Ladies' Blouses and Sweaters

American	10	12	14	16	18	20
Continental	38	40	42	44	46	48
British	32	34	36	38	40	42

Ladies' Hosiery

American	8	8.5	9	9.5	10	10.5
Continental	1	2	3	4	5	6
British	8	8.5	9	9.5	10	10.5

Ladies' Shoes

American	5	6	7	8	9	10
Continental	36	37	38	39	40	41
British	3.5	4.5	5.5	6.5	7.5	8.5

Men's Suits

American	34	36	38	40	42	44	46	48
Continental	44	46	48	50	52	54	56	58
British	34	36	38	40	42	44	46	48

Men's Shirts

American	14	15	15.5	16	16.5	17	17.5	18
Continental	37	38	39	41	42	43	44	45
British	14	15	15.5	16	16	17	17.5	18

Men's Shoes

American	7	8	9	10	11	12	13
Continental	39.5	41	42	43	44.5	46	47
British	6	7	8	9	10	11	12

Alphabetical Store Directory

1887 Dance Shoppe

Professional dancers, moms dressing their petite princess-es, and self-proclaimed sugarplum fairies delight their inner ballerinas with this glittery barrage of ballet and dance essentials. Setting the stage are tutus, tiaras, legwarmers, dance shoes, tights, jazz pants, and flamboyant flamenco outfits by tried-and-true brand names like Repetto, Mondor, Danskin, Capezio and Bloch.

Cow Hollow	**415-441-1887**
2206 Union Street	Daily 10-6:30 (Sun 11-4:30)
San Francisco 94123	

☆ A Girl and Her Dog

Yupscale style hounds in Noe Valley were thrilled when Annette Hickey and her Yorkshire terrier bounded into the 'hood. The former buyer for bebe has a penchant for all things pretty (think Rebecca Taylor, Development, Diane von Furstenberg) and presents them with bags, hats and a few boots in her gently-edgy pistachio-splashed place. Vinyl shower curtains deck the corrugated metal dressing-rooms and the steel displays are on casters, all the better to vary the layout when a new shipment arrives…which is often.

Noe Valley	**415-643-0346**
3932 24th Street	Mon-Fri 11-7, Sat-Sun 11-6
San Francisco 94114	

A Motion Studio

Contemporary streetwear fans who dig discovery should seek out this underground SoMa space for its unique and super-affordable clothing. AMS's real biz is producing sample lines and product development for Bay Area big shots like bebe, which explains the cutting machines and pattern tables scattered about and their own offbeat fashion made from fabric remnants. Don't miss the DJ-spinning soirees where AMS's lines, Hieros (men) and Fire (women), are debuted each month. Also find other local indie talent at this raw industrial shop. Check their website for the latest styles, and when you're in the 'hood look for the orange jacket hanging outside the door. www.amotionstudio.com

SoMa	**415-957-1411**
440 Brannan Street	Tues-Sun 12-7
San Francisco 94107	

A Pea in the Pod

Expecting mothers who don't expect to put their careers on hold love this upscale maternity stop. The pricey pregnant attire and other stuff with stretch—Lilly Pulitzer, ABS, Vivienne Tam, Nicole Miller, Tahari, Seven Jeans, Riley—has office-goers who are showing, showing up in style. Look for great basics—shifts, jackets and other non-restrictive and roomy essentials—plus A Pea's own maternity thong. www.apeainthepod.com

Union Square	**415-391-1400**
290 Sutter Street	Daily 10-6 (Sun 11-5)
San Francisco 94108	

A/X Armani Exchange

The more budget-minded Armani adherents flock here for his lowest-priced collection: basics with a bit of gloss and shine. Cap-sleeve crews, cropped jackets, indie denims and drawstring pants are just some of the styles that make this Italian Gap-like place a little more groovy. Everything comes in cutting-edge cloths, urban interpretations for the young and street-savvy. www.armaniexchange.com

Cow Hollow   **415-749-0891**
2090 Union Street   Daily 10-8 (Sun 11-6)
San Francisco 94123

Peninsula   **650-325-7583**
Stanford Shopping Center   Mon-Fri 10-9
Palo Alto 94304   Sat 10-7, Sun 11-6

Aaardvarks

Raging for retro? Turn to LA-based Aaardvarks, a second-hand institution that opened for business in Hollywood in 1972 and now boasts six locales. The Haight store debuted in 1980 stocking the kind of vintage frocks, bowling shirts, dinner jackets and petticoats that satisfy those obsessed with eras gone by. According to one sales clerk, "We specialize in everything," and that's just how the thrifty place looks.

Haight-Ashbury   **415-621-3141**
1501 Haight Street   Daily 11-7
San Francisco 94117

☆ Ab Fits

Bay Area trendmeisters trek to this royal purple and red outpost in North Beach for its happening apparel and perfectly unpretentious vibe. The downtown-looking shop attracts a funky uptown, cash-happy crowd who cruise in for Ab's fab jeans (Paper Denim & Cloth, SBU, AG, Seven, Rogan) and hipster clothing from lines like Paul & Joe, Rozae Nichols, Etro, Burning Torch, William Reid, Autumn Cashmere, Nanette Lepore and RA.RE.

North Beach   **415-982-5726**
1519 Grant Avenue   Tues-Sat 11-6:30, Sun 12-6
San Francisco 94133

Abercrombie & Fitch

Young style-setters in search of a six-pack stomach like the ones featured in *A&F Quarterly*, the company's racy magalog, crave the all-American-meets-outdoor-utilitarian wares that make the models look so steamy. The once stuffy outdoor outfitter, now over a century old, turns out all the graphic tees, nylon pants, surf shorts and tropical bikinis needed to keep them on the casual cutting edge. Don't miss the stores for kids. www.abercrombie.com and www.abercrombiekids.com

Union Square   **415-284-9276**
San Francisco Shopping Centre   Daily 9:30-8 (Sun 11-6)
865 Market Street   San Francisco 94104

Sunset   **415-664-3091**
Stonestown Galleria   Daily 10-8 (Sun 11-6)
3251 20th Avenue   San Francisco 94132

☆ Abigail Morgan   👤

Pacific Heights preppies with pizzazz love this Victorian-apartment-turned-boutique where shopping feels like browsing in a friend's closet. One room houses higher-end lines like Alice+Olivia and Helen Wang, another sports Zoë SF activewear, loungewear and lingerie, and a third showcases accessories and jewelry by local designers. Don't stop in without trying something on—the extra large dressing-rooms made from vintage doors and ticking stripe curtains are like stepping into a very special summer beach cabana.   www.abigailmorgan.com

Cow Hollow   **415-567-1779**
1640 Union Street   Sun-Mon 12-5, Tues-Sat 11-7
San Francisco 94123

Aerosoles   👤

Packed with Union Square pedestrians pining for cheap and chic soles, this surprisingly popular spot feeds a no-fuss fashion crowd that cares about comfort. Suit up or dress down with these practical pumps, strappy slingbacks, cork-embossed heels and slides of every fashion imaginable, all to be had at an unreal value.   www.aerosoles.com

Union Square   **415-986-8890**
414 Sutter Street   Daily10-7 (Sun 11-6)
San Francisco 94108

agnès b.   👤👤👤

Followers of this French designer fall for her emphatic feminine touch, carefree cuts for men and touches of the season's top trends. Staples include stripes and dots (an agnès b. signature), charming trenches, cropped cardigans, a rainbow of T-shirts and reliable suits in crisp cottons and easy-to-wear rayon. The cool, clean collections, plus the irresistible kids' line, are perfect work and playwear for any fashion-wise francophile.   www.agnesb.fr

Union Square   **415-772-9995**
33 Grant Avenue   Daily 11-7 (Sun 11-6)
San Francisco 94108

Alaya   👤

The peaceful vibe of inner Sunset's destination boutique could be attributed to its beginnings as the S.F. Zen Center's shop for meditation mats and pull-on pants. But in 1985 Karin Gjording stretched the soothing offerings to include comfortable, classic/contemporary womenswear. Brands like Blue Dot, Michael Stars, Flax, Citron and Christopher Blue complement accessories and a legendary long scarf selection.

Sunset   **415-731-2681**
1256 9th Avenue   Mon-Fri 10:30-6:30
San Francisco 94122   Sat 10-6, Sun 12-5

The Alden Shop

Their roots go back to 1884, but gentlemanly old-school soles have been selling at this particular, somewhat sober store since 1970. Hand-worked oxfords, brogues and simple leather slip-ons make up the traditional stock, in addition to a small selection of slightly more updated numbers. It's the classics that count here, outfitting dandies and more mature suits from the nearby financial district. www.aldenshop.com

Union Square   415-421-6691
201 Kearny Street   Mon-Sat 10-6
San Francisco 94108

Aldo

For pure attitude at affordable prices, Aldo is a wise footwear choice. Peddling the latest tread trends, watered-down but just as up-to-date as runway walkers (think wild wedges, wooden soles, sassy slides), this shoe source is sure to please those on a budget. Aldo Bensadoun's Canadian company is an urban mall rat's favorite find.   www.aldoshoes.com

Union Square   415-989-2544
844 Market Street   Daily 9:30-8 (Sun 11-7)
San Francisco 94102

Sunset   415 566-0560
Stonestown Galleria   Daily 10-9 (Sun 11-6)
3251 20th Avenue   San Francisco 94132

☆ Alençon Couture Bridal

Self-taught designer Nancy Taylor started her couture bridal company in 1989. Today her stunning European and period-influenced styles do brisk business with celebs, socialites and fiancées of Nor Cal's powerpeople. Taylor, who made Abra Berman her partner in 2000, more than succeeds in her attempt at "a couture look that's taken more from evening-wear and translated into bridal".   www.alencon-bridal.com

Marin   415-389-9408
318 Miller Avenue   (by appointment only)
Mill Valley 94941

Alfred Dunhill

Celebrated for cigars, this distinguished dealer of English luxe also boasts an entire world of classy suits, shirts, ties and sportswear. No matter what your preference, off the rack or custom-made, count on a refined taste of gentleman's classics.

Union Square   415-781-3368
250 Post Street   Daily 9-6 (Sun 12-5)
San Francisco 94108

All American Boy

Situated in the Castro quartier for over a quarter of a century, All American Boy caters to, well, the all-American boy who digs a decent pair of denim (Dickies, Buffalo Denim), polos and button-down shirts (Forecast) and a crazier hit of club clothes (Greg Parry). The small store also packs in plenty of activewear—from Speedos to board shorts—SF- and Castro-emblazoned sweatshirts and a popular All American Boy line of tees, tanks and caps.

Castro   **415-861-0444**
463 Castro Street   Daily 10-9 (Sun 11-7)
San Francisco 94114

☆ Alla Prima

Calling all lingerie lovers. Alla Prima is one of the best boutiques in town for boudoir booty—a one-stop shop for upscale undergarments. It's an easy environment for the more modest, not to mention males on a mission, looking to pick up special pieces. Cosabella's cozy thongs line up near La Perla, Aubade, Venuss, Khurana, Lise Charmel and Only Hearts bras, boylegs and lacy legwear. The Hayes Street store also sells swimwear upstairs.

Hayes Valley   **415-864-8180**
539 Hayes Street   Daily 11-7 (Sun 12-5)
San Francisco 94102

North Beach   **415-397-4077**
1420 Grant Avenue   Tues-Sat 11-7, Sun 12-5
San Francisco 94133

Allen Edmonds

Conservative types can't get enough of this far-from-trendy footwear. The traditional slip-on loafers, lace-ups, oxfords and tasseled moccasins come in basic browns and black, woven, formal, casual and fussy-free. Along with sturdier boots, belts and wallets, these shoes keep downtown suit-lovers on their classic toes.   www.allenedmonds.com

Union Square   **415-391-4545**
171 Post Street   Mon-Fri 9-7, Sat 9-6, Sun 11-6
San Francisco 94108

Alternative Design Studio

This tiny space just off the Mission's main shopping artery is home to over 1,000 hat designs, mostly from owner/milliner Elina Davenport. She and husband, Isaac, hawk every hat shape imaginable, from casual roll-ups to flapper's cloche, in hemp, knit, faux fur, straw and soft stretchy fabrics. Caps of any kind can be custom ordered. Davenport has also become the source for comfy, attractive and affordable hats designed for women experiencing hair loss.   www.adshats.com

Mission   **415-255-2787**
3458 18th Street   Wed-Sun 12-6
San Francisco 94110

AMA

When the fashionably fearless want to make a sultry statement they turn to this Italian-import shop for bold belts, noticeable necklaces, girly purses, clingy camisoles and playful hair accessories. Think Italy's answer to seductive St. Tropez with colorful fashions to match.

Marina   **415-345-1090**
2276 Chestnut Street   Mon-Fri 10-8, Sat-Sun 10-7
San Francisco 94123

Ambiance

Dress selects are why young women whiz in and out of Ambiance, a small specialty chain that doesn't look like much. Jammed with everything from shoes to vintage lamps, the three locales also rack up flowery, frilly and refined dresses from lines like Betsey Johnson, Trina Turk, Tessuto, French Connection and XOXO. Find full-length formals perfect for the prom at the Haight Street store.

Haight-Ashbury   **415-552-5095**
1458 Haight Street   Mon-Sat 10-7, Sun 11-7 (winter)
San Francisco 94117   Mon-Sat 10-8, Sun 11-8 (summer)

Cow Hollow   **415-923-9797**
1864 Union Street   Mon-Fri 11-7, Sat 10-7, Sun 11-6
San Francisco 94123

Noe Valley   **415-647-7144**
3985 24th Street   Mon-Fri 11-7, Sat 10-6, Sun 11-6
San Francisco 94114

American Eagle Outfitters

A collegiate crew paying homage to *Dawson's Creek* (whose cast comes clad in AE) can't get enough of the splashy halters, cool cargos, graphic tees, board shorts, shoes and bikinis at this relaxed retailer. Young, clean-cut kids and adult kids alike live in this wholesome, affordable and all-American apparel.   www.ae.com

Union Square   **415-543-4550**
San Francisco Shopping Centre   Mon-Sat 9:30-8, Sun 11-7
865 Market Street   San Francisco 94103

☆ American Rag Cie

Fashionistas fond of the old and the new drool over the mouthwatering merchandise at this warehousey institution. Owners Mark and Margot Wertz split their airy place in two—couturish contemporary duds (Jill Stuart, Juicy Couture, Paper Denim, Seven, Jeremy Scott, Paul & Joe) on one side, European vintage on the other. A mod assort-ment of shoes monopolizes the middle (Clone, Clarks, Diesel, Marc Jacobs).

Nob Hill   **415-474-5214**
1305 Van Ness Avenue   Daily 10-9 (Sun 12-7)
San Francisco 94109

Ann Taylor

Career crunchers, conservative lunchers and countryside cruisers bow to their tried-and-true AT. She'll take you from breakfast to the bureau and out to a brasserie or bar in understated, all-American style. Find everything from suits to separates and sportswear, private-label soles, a great petite corner and incredible sales.   www.anntaylor.com

Union Square 415-543-2487
San Francisco Shopping Centre Mon-Sat 9:30-8
865 Market Street Sun 11-6
San Francisco 94103

Union Square 415-788-0716
240 Post Street Mon-Sat 10-7
San Francisco 94108 Sun 12-6

Financial District 415-989-5355
3 Embarcadero Center Mon-Fri 10-7, Sat 11-7
San Francisco 94111 Sun 11-5

Ghirardelli Square 415-775-2872
900 North Point Street Mon-Thurs 10-6
San Francisco 94109 Fri-Sat 10-7, Sun 11-6

Sunset 415-564-0229
Stonestown Galleria Daily 10-9 (Sun 11-6)
3251 20th Avenue San Francisco 94132

Ann Taylor Loft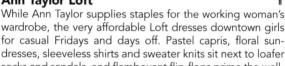

While Ann Taylor supplies staples for the working woman's wardrobe, the very affordable Loft dresses downtown girls for casual Fridays and days off. Pastel capris, floral sundresses, sleeveless shirts and sweater knits sit next to loafer socks and sandals, and flamboyant flip-flops prime the well-preened girl-next-door for color-coordinated fun.

Union Square 415-576-1588
246 Sutter Street Daily 10-8 (Sun 11-7)
San Francisco 94108

Marin 415-945-9215
100 Corte Madera Town Center Mon-Fri 10-9
Corte Madera 94925 Sat-Sun 11-6

Annies

After years as this store's buyer/manager, Suzanne Stevens stepped up to a new role as owner. Fashionistas still count on her to provide their up-to-the-second fashion fix for the latest from Development, Marc by Marc Jacobs, Citizens of Humanity and Seven Jeans. To meet the needs of the stylish moms-to-be, Stevens recently added a maternity corner to the shop featuring Cadau, Liz Lange and Diane von Furstenberg. And coming soon is a menswear corner, appropriately nicknamed "Mannies". www.anniesclothing.com

Pacific Heights 415-292-7164
2512 Sacramento Street Tues-Sat 11-7
San Francisco 94115 Sun 12-5, Monday by appointment

Anthropologie

Outgrown Urban Outfitters? Don't despair. More mature style mavens past their teenage prime can dig into all the trendy trappings at this grown-up outpost where jeans, tees and teapots all meet. The vast depots are just like general stores (better, in fact), mixing home-furnishing finds plucked from faraway lands and flea markets with store-designed repros and urban-chic clothing—lots of denim and lines like Work Order, Plenty, Men at Lappore, Maxou and Anthro's own label. www.anthropologie.com

Union Square **415-434-2210**
880 Market Street Daily 10-8 (Sun 11-7)
San Francisco 94102

Any Mountain

This adventurewear supermarket keeps Silicon Valley outdoor addicts in stylish shape. Launched in 1972 as an alpine ski shop on the Peninsula, it's a specialty chain selling ski and snowboard gear and apparel fit for the slopes. Also find clothing for camping, hiking and general adventure travel, from lines like White Sierra, Patagonia and Columbia. www.anymountaingear.com

Tenderloin **415-345-8080**
2598 Taylor Street Mon-Fri 10-9
San Francisco 94133 Sat 10-6, Sun 11-6

Berkeley **510-665-3939**
2777 Shattuck Avenue Mon-Fri 10-9, Sat 10-6, Sun 11-6
Berkeley 94705

Marin **415-927-0170**
71 Tamal Vista Boulevard Mon-Fri 10-9
Corte Madera 94925 Sat 10-6, Sun 11-6

Peninsula **650-361-1213**
928 Whipple Avenue Mon-Wed 11-7
Redwood City 94063 Sat 10-6, Sun 11-6

April in Paris

Hermès disciple Beatrice Amblard spent 14 years with the French luxury goods house. Now, out of her out-of-the-way salon, this leather specialist is serving up her own designs: custom-crafted bags, belts, wallets and briefcases—classic turns of exotic and sometimes mixed skins from alligator to ostrich. Spot her satchels by the 18-karat bumblebee stamped on the flap. Kelly bags beware.

Richmond **415-750-9910**
55 Clement Street Tues-Sat 10-5
San Francisco 94118 (also by appointment)

Arden B.

One notch up from Wet Seal's teenage temple, this mall-perfect store brings trendy to women's sizes, proving you don't need to be a Junior to stay on top of the latest fads and fashion. Low-riding denim, fitted tanks, sheer tops, and knee-length skirts—a must-stop for single-season keepers. www.wetseal.com

Union Square **415-777-1691**
San Francisco Shopping Centre Daily 9:30-8 (Sun 11-6)
865 Market Street San Francisco 941032

Aricie

High-powered hotties hustle to this bodacious boutique for luxe lingerie from Lise Charmel, Aubade and Cotton Club.

Even the pink neon skirting the walls can't contend with the colorful lace bras and bottoms, waist-wincing corsets, silk robes and nighties and silk stockings perfect for every seductive siren.

Union Square
Crocker Galleria, 50 Post Street
San Francisco 94104

415-989-0261
Mon-Fri 10-6, Sat 10-5

Arthur Beren Shoes

Take the shoe department out of a department store and you'd have something similar to Beren Shoes. This corner shop on the east side of the square sells a melee of natty heels, lovely loafers and snazzy sandals from big-name designers like Ferragamo, Robert Clergerie, Stuart Weitzman, Prada Sport and Cole Haan. www.berenshoes.com

Union Square
222 Stockton Street
San Francisco 94108

415-397-8900
Mon-Fri 9:30-7, Sat 9:30-6
Sun 12-6

Astrid's Rabat Shoes & Accessories

Once affiliated with Rabat down the street (well, back in 1979), Astrid's Rabat carved its own niche, concentrating on footwear in a more comfortable and practical fashion. This low-key shop catalogs everything from clogs to Clarks to Converse with echoes of ecco, Bass, Dansko and Frye. www.astrids-rabat-shoes.com

Noe Valley
3909 24th Street
San Francisco 94114

415-282-7400
Mon-Fri 11-6:30
Sat 10-6:30, Sun 11-6

Atelier des Modistes

One of the few clothing merchants in rich Russian Hill, this bridal and couture favorite sells the exclusive designs of Suzanne Hanley, who cuts and sews her pricey pieces in back. Find elegant gowns in Italian silk satins and shantung, trimmed in vintage French trappings or beaded with pearls, emeralds and other precious and semi-precious stones. www.atelierdesmodistes.com

Russian Hill
1903 Hyde Street
San Francisco 94109

415-775-0545
Wed-Sat 12-8

Azadeh

Union Street has such a massive crop of shops, it's easy to miss Azadeh's upstairs atelier. But if you're the kind who covets custom-made curvy gowns with extra trimmings (especially for bridal and special occasions), this Persian designer is worth a try. Choose from off-the-rack styles (she also has an rtw collection) or an original creation; the salespeople are uber-accommodating. Look for custom swimwear and accessories too. www.azadehstudio.com

Cow Hollow
2066 Union Street
San Francisco 94123

415-292-9898
Mon-Fri 10:30-7
Sat 11-6, Sun 12-5

Babette

Now that the droves of dot-commers have departed from the neighborhood, Babette Pinsky can focus on the more serious shoppers who sift through her pleated and crinkled tops and skirts (à la Issey Miyake) and signature outerwear, all in innovative high-tech textiles. The store also carries jeans from Cambio and leather bags from Hester van Eeghen. www.babettesf.com

SoMa 415-267-0282
92 South Park Mon-Fri 10-5, Sat 11-5
San Francisco 94107

North Beach 415-986-1174
1400 Grant Avenue Mon-Fri 11-7
San Francisco 94133 Sat 11-6, Sun 12-5

Directory

Banana Republic

Step into Gap's big brother for a shirt and you're more likely to walk out with blue bags stuffed with a wardrobe of essentials. It's tough to resist the goodies so modly stocked here—khakis, suits, sundresses, socks and general dress-down workwear that seamlessly takes you from brunch to boardroom in millennium mode. www.bananarepublic.com

Union Square 415-788-3087
256 Grant Avenue Daily 10-8 (Sun 11-7)
San Francisco 94108

Financial District 415-986-5076
2 Embarcadero Center Mon-Fri 10-7, Sat 12-6
San Francisco 94111 Sun 12-5

Sunset 415-753-3330
Stonestown Galleria Daily 10-9 (Sun 11-6)
3251 20th Avenue San Francisco 94132

Marin 415-383-4900
59 Throckmorton Avenue Daily 10-7 (Sun 11-6)
Mill Valley 94941

Marin 415-924-3330
Village at Corte Madera Mon-Fri 10-9
1702 Redwood Highway Sat 10-7:30, Sun 11-6
Corte Madera 94925

☆ The Bar

Catering to the well-heeled and well-paid, this elegantly edgy boutique has offered an articulate aggregate of fashions suitable for strolling upscale Sacramento Street or attending opening night at the Opera since its mid-2001 opening. Owner Andrea Schnitzer, who's a partner at neighboring footwear favorite Fetish, perks up the shopping party with designs by Megan Park, Alberta Ferretti, Lela Rose and Paul Smith, as well as oversized couches and free lattes and cappuccinos.

Presidio Heights 415-409-4901
340 Presidio Avenue Daily 10-6 (Sun 12-5)
San Francisco 94115

Barcelino

Genteel gentlemen (and, in one of the stores, women) with a taste for fine Italian clothes frequent these boutiques, three of them right on the fringe of the financial district. Meticulous tailoring, ties, shoes, hats, ascots and sport jackets are all part of the polished and smart selection.   www.barcelino.com

Union Square   **415-781-5777**
498 Post Street   Daily 10-7 (Sun 11-6)
San Francisco 94102

Union Square   **415-273-2800**
Crocker Galleria   Mon-Fri 10-6, Sat 10-5
50 Post Street   San Francisco 94104

Union Square (W)   **415-912-5700**
476 Post Street   Daily 10-7 (Sun 11-6)
San Francisco 94102

Peninsula   **650-326-9170**
Stanford Shopping Center   Mon-Fri 9:30-9
Palo Alto 94304   Sat 9:30-7, Sun 10-6

☆ Baxter Hull

Former Bertram Mann employee Matt Hull now runs this retail shop showcasing outdoor-inspired Bertram Mann goods along with other performance-based lines such as Horny Toad and Gramicci. From fluffy, funky fleece to raingear, cotton crushers and luggage and bags, everything is made from high-quality industrial-strength fabrics in a great range of colors. This answer to more familiar outdoorwear makes L.L.Bean look tragically unhip.   www.baxterhull.com

Pacific Heights   **415-931-8773**
1906 Fillmore Street   Tues-Sat 11-7
San Francisco 94115   Sun 12-6

BCBG max azria

LA-based fashion entrepreneur Max Azria swears by the sexy, the swanky and the stylishly spirited—after all, BCBG (bon chic bon genre) is French slang for well-dressed yuppie. He's a pro at translating trends and serving them up at mouth-watering prices, and sends a fresh set of designs (especially dresses) to his stores each month. This universe of euro-sophistication and American attitude also includes eyewear, swimwear and underwear, plus a bevy of accessories.

Union Square   **415-362-7360**
331 Powell Street   Mon-Sat 10-8
San Francisco 94102   Sun 11-6

Union Square   **415-284-9373**
San Francisco Shopping Centre   Daily 9:30-8 (Sun 11-6)
865 Market Street   San Francisco 94103

Bebe

Body-conscious babes rummaging for runway looks at prices that don't really dent the purse turn to bebe. And who doesn't want to look like the sexy sirens splattered across bus stops and billboards? This San Francisco company takes care of a trendy gal's entire wardrobe—from breakfast to bureau to bar—with a whole world of active, outer, sports and cocktailwear.   www.bebe.com

Pacific Heights   **415-771-2323**
2133 Fillmore Street   Mon-Fri 10-7, Sat 10-6, Sun 11-6
San Francisco 94115

Union Square   **415-781-2323**
21 Grant Avenue   Mon-Fri 10-7, Sat 10-6, Sun 12-6
San Francisco 94108

Union Square   **415-543-1794**
San Francisco Shopping Centre   Mon-Sat 9:30-8, Sun 11-6
865 Market Street   San Francisco 94103

Sunset   **415-242-3303**
Stonestown Galleria   Daily 10-9 (Sun 11-6)
3251 20th Avenue   San Francisco 94132

Cow Hollow   **415-563-2323**
2095 Union Street   Daily 10-8 (Sun 11-6)
San Francisco 94123

Marin   **415-924-0213**
Village at Corte Madera   Mon-Fri 10-9, Sat 10-7:30
1720 Redwood Highway   Sun 11-6
Corte Madera 94925

Peninsula   **650-321-2323**
Stanford Shopping Center   Mon-Fri 10-9, Sat 10-7
Palo Alto 94304   Sun 11-6

☆ Behind the Post Office

Betwixt the tie-dye and touristwear, this little gem is a sure thing for all that's down-to-earth, trendy and chic. With an eye for young and emerging designers—"whatever's original and different"—owner Kim Baskind bets on lines like Development, Katayone Adeli, Ella Moss, Michael Stars and Seven. Fashion fiends have been sniffing out her stylish selects (find shoes, denim and accessories too) for over a decade. Leave your attitude at the door; this place is a pleaser thanks to its easygoing vibe.

Haight-Ashbury   **415-861-2507**
1510 Haight Street   Daily 11-7
San Francisco 94117

Benetton

Although they have over 6,000 stores worldwide, Benetton have long had a quiet California presence (not counting their outspoken advertising and forward-thinking *Colors* magazine). But the new two-story superstore on Stockton Street is making noise. This is the new destination for nonchalant knits, cute cardigans, capris and simple cotton pants and tees, for the entire famiglia from tiny tots to older gents. Also find suits and career garb.

Union Square   **415-979-0533**
San Francisco Shopping Centre   Mon-Sat 9:30-8
865 Market Street   Sun 10:30-6
San Francisco 94103

Union Square

39 Stockton Street

San Francisco 94103

n/a at press time

Daily 10:30-7:30

Peninsula

Stanford Shopping Center

Palo Alto 94303

650-327-1415

Mon-Fri 10-9, Sat 10-7

Sun 11-6

Betsey Johnson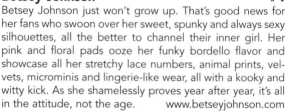

Betsey Johnson just won't grow up. That's good news for her fans who swoon over her sweet, spunky and always sexy silhouettes, all the better to channel their inner girl. Her pink and floral pads ooze her funky bordello flavor and showcase all her stretchy lace numbers, animal prints, velvets, microminis and lingerie-like wear, all with a kooky and witty kick. As she shamelessly proves year after year, it's all in the attitude, not the age.   www.betseyjohnson.com

Union Square

160 Geary Street

San Francisco 94108

415-398-2516

Daily 10-6 (Sun 12-6)

Pacific Heights

2031 Fillmore Street

San Francisco 94115

415-567-2726

Daily 11-7 (Sun 12-6)

Bettina

A favorite Presidio Heights stop for ladies looking for sleek and chic. Trustworthy for trends, owner Doretta Boehm fills her cool chasm with all the right pieces to outfit yuppies and techies in vogue. Prices, though not preposterous, are above average, but the locally well-heeled have no problem dipping into their totes for a touch of Theory, Development, Katayone Adeli and precious jewels from local artists Betsy Barron and Andrea Eve.   www.bettinasf.com

Presidio Heights

3654 Sacramento Street

San Francisco 94118

415-563-8002

Mon-Fri 10:30-6:30

Sat 10:30-6, Sun 12-4

BillyBlue

Men looking to dodge department store grandness opt for this small specialty store. Billy Bragman suits up dapper execs and the classic set who come for the beautiful blazers, reliable tailoring, first-class cashmeres and topcoats in a starched but sociable setting. Names like Vestimenta, Zanella, Trussini and Eton dress shirts are all part of Bragman's fashion band.   www.billyblue.com

Union Square

54 Geary Street

San Francisco 94108

415-781-2111

Mon-Sat 10-6

Birkenstock SF

The crunchy-granola slip-on has made major footway in recent years, with a more fashion-savvy sense, cooler colors and a heel-clicking effort in design. Traditionalists, however, need not despair—amidst all the splashy hues and edgier styles (metallics, reptile prints and slender straps), the iconic foot-forming sandal is still the tried-and-true choice of everyone from West Coast yogis to beach bums and college kids. Take a break with an Odwalla at the store's healthy café. www.birkenstock.com

Union Square 415-989-2475
42 Stockton Street Daily 10-7 (Sun 11-6)
San Francisco 94104

Oakland 510-658-9742
6012 College Avenue Daily 10-6
Oakland 94618

Bloomingdale's

For now, the only piece of Bloomies northern Californians can get is in Palo Alto—perfect for the Silicon Valley set, who love the compact version of Manhattan's 59th-Street store. They find plenty of bridge-priced merchandise from a huge selection of designers, some with a more contemporary twist, in addition to extensive plus-size and petite departments. "It's like no other store in the world," says the slogan, and with its innovative merchandising savvy, offbeat special events and famous little brown bags, perhaps it's right. Look for a blooming new addition to Union Square in the near future. www.bloomingdales.com

Peninsula 650-463-2000
Stanford Shopping Center Mon-Fri 10-9, Sat 10-8
Palo Alto 94304 Sun 11-7

☆ Blu

Cielo's little sister is yet another hot stop on the SF style circuit. Less costly and a tad less serious than its up-the-street sibling, Blu boasts a fashionista's favorite staples: Y-3, Cacharel, Barbara Bui, Marithé & Francois Girbaud, Isabel Marant and other young and edgy items. This corner cruiser with the big metal door also carries a stable of styling shoes, from Clone to Blu Girl.

Pacific Heights 415-776-0643
2259 Fillmore Street Daily 11-7 (Sun 12-6)
San Francisco 94115

Body Body Wear

Toronto designer Stephen Sandler turned up in the Bay Area in 2000 with this smart shop, selling all his body-conscious, cutting-edge cuts. Many a swanky San Franciscan suits up for the club scene in his casual fashion-forward style, which comes in trendy colors and plenty of nylon. BBW duds include cool tees, pants and hooded V-necks, as well as an athletic line of workout pants, muscle tops and tanks. Penny-pinchers take note: most items in the store are under $100. www.bodybodywear.com

Castro 415-621-1223
535 Castro Street Daily 11-7
San Francisco 94114

Body Options

All manner of bodywear with ultra-stretchy seams makes its way onto the racks of this popular chain with 13 stores in the Bay Area. Yoginis om to the City Lights looks, dancers love the Danskin duds and all-around active types go for the Fila, Champion and Adidas garb. There is also a rainbow of tank tops, rayon pants and slinky skirts for sporty slackers who still like a good stretch.

Marina   **415-567-1122**
2108 Chestnut Street   Mon-Sat 10-7, Sun 10-6 (winter)
San Francisco 94123   Mon-Fri 10-8, Sat 10-7
                                                        Sun 11-6 (summer)

Sunset   **415-566-1566**
Stonestown Galleria   Daily 10-9 (Sun 11-6)
3251 20th Avenue   San Francisco 94132

Pacific Heights   **415-567-2085**
2216 Fillmore Street   Mon-Fri 10-8, Sat 10-7
San Francisco 94115   Sun 11-6

Cow Hollow   **415-776-9426**
2100 Union Street   Daily 10-7 (Sun 11-6)
San Francisco 94123

Berkeley   **510-595-8101**
3212 College Avenue   Mon-Sat 10-6, Sun 11-5
Berkeley 94705

Oakland   **510-339-3796**
2056 Mountain Boulevard   Daily 10-6 (Sun 11-5)
Oakland 94611

Body/Citizen

A sporty and dope set covet all the cool wares at this activewear outpost. Jamming tunes fill the two-story scene where the Castro crowd files in for the latest Puma treads, skimpy Speedo suits, Kangol caps and happening Adidas garb. For off-court, post-game fashion needs, check out sibling store Citizen around the corner.www.bodyclothing.com

Castro   **415-861-6111**
4071 18th Street   Daily 11-8 (Sun 11-7)
San Francisco 94114

Bombay Bazaar/Bombay Sari Palace

San Francisco's very own passage to India, this colorful, tandoori-spiced store sells all the traditional trappings from the faraway land. Among the naan, groceries, incense, soaps and many-mirrored Rajasthan accessories sits a sweet selection of vibrant saris, Punjabi suits and shalwar-kamiz. A la mode henna kits and tubes are also available.

Mission   **415-703-0978**
548 Valencia Street   Tues-Sun 10:30-7:15
San Francisco 94110

Bottega Veneta

With all the luxury leather houses loosening up their traditionally tight collars, BV was bound for a major overhaul. And with its recent acquisition by the Gucci group that's just what it got, in the form of high-energy attitude and attention-grabbing colors. The resuscitated rtw collection, crammed with leather tunics, washed denim, zippy coats and its signature woven hide (from headphones to ponytail holders), is back on the map. But, oh, those bags…they're bolder, brighter and woven better than ever.   www.bottegaveneta.com

Union Square   **415-981-1700**
108 Geary Street   Mon-Sat 10-6
San Francisco 94108

Boutique Here

Formerly known as Bisou Bisou, this store underwent an identity change once designer Michele Bohbot started creating a low-end line with the same name for JC Penney. This shop still sells her Bisou Jeans line along with up-and-coming lines such as Hippie, Free People and Brazilian Jeans. A brilliant blend of Bohbot's French roots and LA lifestyle still factor into the sassy stretch dresses, suede-cut minis, sandals, swimwear and lingerie, all at digestible prices.

Cow Hollow   **415-775-1633**
2116 Union Street   Mon-Thurs 11-7
San Francisco 94123   Fri-Sat 11-8, Sun 11-6

Brooks Brothers

Souped up for the millennium, this traditional business, once peddler-in-chief of the preppy uniform, busted out of its Ivy League blue blazer and khaki convention. It is now a contemporary store, complete with CD listening station, coffee-table books and a look that says "J. Crew watch out," selling all the youth-infused fashion that has put BB back in the basics ballgame. Find colorful T-shirts, stretch suits, ice-cream-colored ties and all-American corduroys, capris and cashmere.   www.brooksbrothers.com

Union Square   **415-397-4500**
150 Post Street   Mon-Fri 9:30-7, Sat 10-6
San Francisco 94108   Sun 11-6

Peninsula   **650-462-0936**
Stanford Shopping Center   Mon-Fri 10-9, Sat 10-7
Palo Alto 94304   Sun 11-6

☆ Brown Eyed Girl

If you think Van Morrison's song of the same name is catchy, wait until you see Danielle Bourhis's boutique. Since its 2000 opening this sweet storefront, set up like a home, has quickly become a top stop for girly garb (Shoshanna, Milly, Ella Moss, Paper Denim & Cloth, CK Bradley), sexy stompers, luscious loungewear, designer laundry detergents, perks for puppy, beautiful baby attire and essentials for the pretty city pad.

Pacific Heights   **415-409-0214**
2999 Washington Street   Daily 11-7 (Sun 12-5)
San Francisco 94115

Bryan Lee

Impulsive buyers swear by this small Union Street boutique where, despite the merchandising mess, there are surprisingly good finds. The place is always swarming with fashion vultures who wouldn't ever think of spending big designer bucks. Look for affordable lines like Maria Bianca Nero, Seven and Poleci for women, G Star, Ike & Dean and Ben Sherman for men, and the ubiquitous French Connection for both.

Cow Hollow   **415-923-9923**
1840 Union Street   Daily 10-7 (Sun 11-6)
San Francisco 94123

Buffalo Exchange

Fancy a closet cleansing? Buffalo Exchange gives you a good excuse. The thrifty recycling chain will acquire your cast-off clothes, especially if they're less than two years old. After the trade, restock on others' used items from Kenneth Cole, Kate Spade, Gucci, vintage Levi's and leather. If you're into rummaging through racks, you can score some good stuff. Best of all, BE donates to local non-profits through the Tokens for Bags program.   www.buffaloexchange.com

Haight-Ashbury   **415-431-7733**
1555 Haight Street   Sun-Thurs 11-7, Fri-Sat 11-8
San Francisco 94117

Nob Hill   **415-346-5726**
1800 Polk Street   Daily 11-7 (Sun 12-6)
San Francisco 94109

Berkeley   **510-644-9202**
2585 Telegraph Avenue   Daily 11-8 (Sun 11-7)
Berkeley 94704

Bulo

Riding on the heels of hip Gimme Shoes (literally—it's just next door), this Hayes Valley shoe stop sells its soles to footwear freaks less label-obsessed. Bulo's styling stash, mostly from Italy, is full of all the square-toed, chunky heels and mod boots that keep the Bay Area's underground walking with attitude. Collections include Aketohn, Roberto del Carlo, Obeline, oxs, Cydwoq and Alberto Fermani.   www.buloshoes.com

Hayes Valley (W)   **415-255-4939**
418 Hayes Street   Daily 11-7 (Sun 12-6)
San Francisco 94102

Hayes Valley (M)   **415-864-3244**
437a Hayes Street   (opening times as above)
San Francisco 94102

Pacific Heights   **415-614-9959**
3044 Fillmore Street   (opening times as above)
San Francisco 94123

Burberry

This bland boutique is badly in need of a facelift to match its current hipped-up and happening collection. Hopefully former Gucci groupie Christopher Bailey who is now creatively behind the booming British business will keep the classic plaid pouring out in cutting-edge style across an ever-increasing range of products. Look for a newly renovated storefront in 2004.

Union Square 415-392-2200
225 Post Street Daily 10-6:30 (Sun 12-6)
San Francisco 94108

Burlington Coat Factory

A surprising blend of department-store selections and mass-market merchandise, this old-time crossbreed offers bargains up to 60% off regular retail. Crammed with career clothes and suits, casualwear and shoes, this roomy place is particularly known for its coats (natch). And with a hefty stock of 10,000-20,000, you can be sure you won't be shivering out the door. www.bcfdirect.com

SoMa 415-495-7234
899 Howard Street Daily 10-8 (Sun 11-7)
San Francisco 94103

Button Down

Walk into this gentleman's wardrobe-like store, complete with hand-loomed rugs and gas-burning fireplace, for a classy dose of classics. With an eye on the buttoned-up type who might want to bust out of his blue blazer and loafers, this longtime Presidio Heights peddler offers up mostly Italian sportswear (think Luciano Barbera, Luigi Borelli, Zanella, Bernard Zins, Allegri), with all the accessories to match. Button Down also designs its own signature button-down cotton shirts. About 30% of the goods are for gals.

Presidio Heights 415-563-1311
3415 Sacramento Street Mon-Sat 10-6
San Francisco 94118

Buu

Located on the city's most eclectic shopping stretch, this tiny temple of taste has a huge following. Style-setter Roxy Buu stocks the front of her boxy space with beauty bits, bathroom products, sleek tableware and design-driven housewares. The back of the shop is devoted to three finely edited racks of the coolest in urban chic—Anja Slint, Seven jeans, Barbara Bui, funky tees and some shoes and bags.

Hayes Valley 415-626-1503
506 Hayes Street Mon-Wed 12-7, Thurs-Sat 11-7
San Francisco 94102 Sun 12-6

By Emily

Pacific Heights brides and formalwear fans swear by this shop for custom designs by Emily Mihal. Her claim to fame is a wide price range (dresses range from the hundreds to the thousands) and very personal attention. Last-minute shoppers can also find a selection of Emily's off-the-rack creations, mostly in silk and many with delicate hand-beading.

Cow Hollow   415-440-0081
2271 Union Street   Tues-Sat 12-6
San Francisco 94123

Cable Car Clothiers

Known as "San Francisco's British Goods Store" this family-owned haberdashery has been in business since
1939, and from the look of it not a thing has changed.
The mahogany display cases (imported from England
when the store first opened) house everything from der-
bies to a dandy's favorite duds and pharmaceutical
pleasures.   www.cablecarclothiers.com

Financial District   415-397-4740
200 Bush Street   Mon-Fri 9-5:30
San Francisco 94104

Cal Surplus

Since 1970 urban dwellers have survived the streets in unisex combat-chic clothing and accessories found at this
straight-up surplus shop. Among the camouflage classics
are utilitarian standbys by Ben Davis and Dickies as well as
Carhartt pants, Kangol hats, berets, an array of wool hats
and gloves, big baggy jackets and an eclectic collection of
military patches and pins.

Haight-Ashbury   415-861-0404
1541 Haight Street   Daily 11-6 (Sun 12-5)
San Francisco 94117

Camper

This Spanish shoe company may have a history dating back
to 1877 but today its name is synonymous with fun contemporary fashion. Most famous for their bowling shoe style
pelotas, the company has a wide range of Mediterranean-
inspired shoes with a twist. The designers think wearing
them should feel like having a funny conversation with yourself—as reflected in designs that sometimes asymetrically
continue from one shoe to the other or soles with poems or
sayings stamped in them.   www.camper.com

Union Square   415-296-1005
33 Grant Avenue   Mon-Sat 10-7
San Francisco 94108   Sun 11-6

Canyon Beachwear

Bathing beauties can't go wrong at this popular swimwear
chain. You-wish-you-all-could-be-California-girl get-ups
are aplenty—barely-there bikinis, titillating triangles and
tankinis of the *Sports Illustrated* kind from over 100
steamy Euro and American faves. There's something to
please the Gottex goddess, Calvin Klein beach-cruiser
and the simple Huit woman in itsy-bitsy to boulder-holder
sizes.   www.canyonbeachwear.com

Cow Hollow   415-885-5070
1728 Union Street   Mon-Fri 10-8, Sat 10-7
San Francisco 94123   Sun 11-6

Marin   **415-459-6335**
634 San Anselmo Avenue   Mon-Fri 11-7, Sat 10-6
San Anselmo 94960   Sun 11-6

Cara Mia

This nondescript stop on the Union Street shopping corridor is actually jammed with European jewels—Fendi bags, Joseph pants, Prada purses, plus Daryl K and Chaiken basics. Owner Caroline Maneatis also carries a colorful mix of Supergas, Jack Rogers sandals and something for the style-conscious career woman. For those who like a fashion-forward assortment without the hip attitude.   www.caramiasf.com

Cow Hollow   **415-922-CARA**
1814 Union Street   Daily 10-9
San Francisco 94123

Directory

Carol Doda's Champagne &
Lace Lingerie Boutique

Tucked behind Union Street storefronts, this offbeat lingerie shop with an unexpected mix of bras, bustiers, panties and teddies is the va-va-vroom baby of celebrated topless star and ex-Condor queen Carol Doda. Find silk thongs and boxers for guys and plenty of good- and bad-girl boudoir booty for gals.   www.caroldoda.com

Cow Hollow   **415-776-6900**
1850 Union Street, #1   Daily 11-6 (Sun 11-5)
San Francisco 94123

Casual Corner

No one was probably more delighted to see "office casual" gain fame than this casual corner. In business here since 1971, this value-conscious emporium has more than enough dresses, suits, tops and slacks to entirely wardrobe an easy crowd without draining their bank accounts.   www.casualcorner.com

Union Square   **415-956-2500**
301 Geary Street   Daily 10-9 (Sun 11-7)
San Francisco 94102

Catnip & Bones

Four-legged window shoppers and their human helpers crowd into this pet accoutrement palace for fashions and totes for Fido. Past tables and shelves teeming with pet paraphernalia is a back nook where creatively designed couriers transport puppy in style and visors are sure to shield your furry friend from the city's whimsical weather.

Marina   **415-359-9100**
2220 Chestnut Street   Daily 10-8 (Sun 10-6)
San Francisco 94123

Chadwicks of London

It's tough to leave these lacy lingerie stops without a little bit of loveliness. The foofy window dressings don't do justice to the first-rate frilliness inside. If you like a small, intimate ambiance when shopping for intimates (think Cosabella, Only Hearts and Rigby & Peller), Chadwicks is your underwear Eden.

Marina 415-775-3423
2068 Chestnut Street Mon-Fri 11-7, Sat 10:30-6
San Francisco 94123 Sun 12-6

Marin 415-388-7704
9 Throckmorton Avenue Mon-Fri 11-6:30, Sat 10:30-6
Mill Valley 94941 Sun 12-6

Marin 415-721-7119
526 San Anselmo Avenue Mon-Fri 11-6, Sat 10:30-6
San Anselmo 94960 Sun 12-6

Chanel ♀

Japanese tourists flock from this boutique armed with bundles of black shopping bags after snatching up all the quilted purses and everything that smacks of the two linked Cs. Designer Karl Lagerfeld successfully serves up twists on the classic tweed suit, reinventions of Coco's little black dress and a chic spin on ski, swim or sunwear season after season, proving that this old French house still reigns as queen of the fashion jungle. www.chanel.com

Union Square 415-981-1550
155 Maiden Lane Daily 10-6 (Sun 12-5)
San Francisco 94108

Charles David ♀

Snappy sandals and more feminine footwear are to be found at this LA-based chain. Designer Nathalie Marciano, daughter of Charles David's founder (Charles Malka) and wife of Guess? chief Maurice Marciano, turns out young-spirited shoes, slides and fab black boots right in step with the trends. Her lines include Guess? footwear and Nathalie M for Charles David. www.charlesdavid.com

Union Square 415-348-9733
San Francisco Shopping Centre Mon-Sat 9:30-8
865 Market Street Sun 11-6
San Francisco 94103

Chico's ♀

Fashion snobs might snub this cheaper-end chain but economically minded shoppers swear by it. The easy-edged emporiums, headquartered in Fort Myers, Florida, hail the sunny southern spirit with hot-weather wear that's well in step with the casual California lifestyle. The company's no-fuss fashion includes classic-cut pants, colorful prints and a world of bright linen blouses, bags, baubles and belts. www.chicos.com

Union Square 415-495-2748
San Francisco Shopping Centre Mon-Sat 9:30-8, Sun 11-6
865 Market Street San Francisco 94103

Sunset
Stonestown Galleria
3251 20th Avenue
415-664-8376
Daily 10-9 (Sun 11-6)
San Francisco 94132

Marin
Village at Corte Madera
1518 Redwood Highway
Corte Madera 94925
415-945-0855
Mon-Fri 10-9, Sat 10-7:30
Sun 11-6

Peninsula
1113 Burlingame Avenue
Burlingame 94014
650-579-4600
Mon-Fri 10-6, Sat 10-7
Sun 12-5

Peninsula
396 University Avenue
Palo Alto 94301
650-321-1850
Mon-Fri 10-7, Sat 10-6
Sun 12-5

Directory

The Children's Place

Tailored for tots with a taste for the trendy, this children's emporium pops with bubble-gum colors, pretty plaids, funky florals and every accessory necessary to give kids' wardrobes some kick. Girls will gawk at decal-donning tees, slick shades and candy-colored capris. Boys head for the hip selection of shirts and slacks in retro patterns.

Union Square
180 Sutter Street
San Francisco 94108
415-434-4737
Daily 9:30-8 (Sun 12-5)

Christian Dior

The tragically hip (and rich) have been hitting this distinguished fashion house ever since cutting-edge guru John Galliano came on board, flaunting his forward-thinking fashion in wild and controversial runway shows. Add ex-YSL designer Hedi Slimane to the Dior stable (for Dior Homme, unfortunately not yet sold at this locale) and you've got a creative force that beckons the glamorati in pursuit of Dior's dynamic street-meets-chic looks. The gray and white stately store houses razor-cut suits, shoes, bias-cut gowns and accessories. www.dior.com

Union Square
216 Stockton Street
San Francisco 94108
415-544-0394
Daily 10-6 (Sun 12-5)

Cicada

One could easily call the dramatic designs at this Zen, fountain-filled, gallery-like space wearable art. Original and eccentric, exotically cut, crimped and in beautiful textiles, the dresses, tops and pants from over 100 "artists" featured here are eye-popping. One-of-a-kind kind of girls, be sure to check out the bridal and couture salon a few doors down for pared-down poofs.

Union Square
547 Sutter Street
San Francisco 94102
415-398-4000
Mon-Sat 10-6

Union Square (bridal)
555 Sutter Street, 4th floor
San Francisco 94102
415-398-4000
Mon-Sat 10-6
(also by appointment)

☆ Cielo

Serious style-setters descend on Cielo when the urge to splurge comes on. Sophisticated, spacious and sleek, the Fillmore high-fashion haven houses heavy-hitting designers like Ann Demeulemeester, Balenciaga, Dries Van Noten, Jean Paul Gaultier and Piazza Sempione. Also find a few selected shoes, accessories and handbags. There's a younger, edgier mix at sibling store Blu up the street.

Pacific Heights
2225 Fillmore Street
San Francisco 94115

415-776-0641
Daily 11-7 (Sun 12-6)

Peninsula
Stanford Shopping Center
Palo Alto 94304

650-329-8833
Mon-Fri 10-9, Sat 10-7
Sun 11-6

Citizen

A mod menswear market that lures all the fashionable boys in the 'hood. Citizen dishes out the top trends from the likes of Energie, Jack Spade, Kenneth Cole, DKNY, Theory, Fred Perry, Paul Frank and French Connection—jeans, undies, tees, shoes and a delicious menu of accessories. Be sure to check out brother boutique Body around the corner for hip athleticwear. www.bodyclothing.com

Castro
536 Castro Street
San Francisco 94114

415-558-9429
Daily 10-8 (Sun 11-7)

City Fitness

Don't be put off by the merchandising mess, this boxy vendor really has a fab fitness-inspired selection. Sport label snobs, stylishly self-conscious, will love the choice of Perfetto, Lom, Pearl Izumi and Danskin. Gals will be distracted by the Cosabella thongs, Michael Stars, Juicy and Petit Bateau T-shirts and all the stretchy streetwear—low-riders, form-fitting denim and pleather pants—all so you can have that post-workout polished look.

Marina
3251 Pierce Street
San Francisco 94123

415-345-9326
Daily 11:30-6 (Sun 12-5)

Clobba

The young and trendy tromp through this small chain in search of seasonal and suitable club gear. Painted pants, animal-print tops, sparkling sweaters and all the clubby trappings—from bags to sunglasses to body-hugging looks—attract night owls in vogue.

Castro
587 Castro Street
San Francisco 94114

415-487-9050
Daily 11-7

Haight-Ashbury
1604 Haight Street
San Francisco 94117

415-864-4701
Daily 11-7

Berkeley   **510-540-5901**
2570 Bancroft Way   Daily 11-7
Berkeley 94704

Club Monaco

What started as a search for the perfect white shirt led a Canadian crew into an affordable emporium business where classic essentials are always on hand. Now the Club Monaco empire includes accessories and cosmetics in addition to its stellar staples—cotton shirts, tweed trousers, chinos, oxford shirts—and trendier runway knock-offs.   www.clubmonaco.com

Union Square   **415-856-0828**
San Francisco Shopping Centre   Daily 9:30-8 (Sun 10-6)
865 Market Street, Suite 110
San Francisco 94108

Coach

Coach has long been a safe and stylish closet staple for even the fashion weary. But now that Reed Krakoff has come along to hip up the brand, the ubiquitous leather bag (in updated shapes, popping prints and a cooler edge) has garnered a must-have status among the fashion elite too. Within the cool Coach kingdom, find the bags, belts and small leather goods to complete any chic wardrobe.

Union Square   **415-392-1772**
190 Post Street   Daily 10-7:30 (Sun 11-6)
San Francisco 94108

Union Square   **415-543-7152**
San Francisco Shopping Centre   Daily 9:30-8 (Sun 11-6)
865 Market Street   San Francisco 94103

Marin   **415-924-5046**
Village at Corte Madera   Mon-Fri 10-9, Sat 10-7:30
1636 Redwood Highway   Sun 11-6
Corte Madera 94925

Peninsula   **650-327-1772**
Stanford Shopping Center   Mon-Fri 10-9, Sat 10-7
Palo Alto 94304   Sun 11-6

Cole Haan

Catering to both young and grown-up traditionalists in search of class-act contemporary calfskins, Cole Haan is all about modern artisanship. Handmade career-worthy footwear comes in the form of luxe loafers, moccasins and Mary Janes, great for a leisurely classic look. Some slides and sandals have been spiced up with visible Nike Air technology. Find also handbags, belts and hosiery.   www.colehaan.com

Union Square   **415-391-1760**
324 Stockton Street   Mon-Sat 10-7 (Thurs 10-8)
San Francisco 94108   Sun 11-6

Coquette

This sweet spot on the shopping stretch of funky-cool Hayes Street is fully of flirty sophisticated finds. Owner

Sabine Hinds describes her collection as "tight, sexy, casual stuff geared toward going out". But the boutique is more likely to inspire one to stay in—and soak up the decidedly New York vibe, local revolving artworks, slow-grooving music and the latest from Cultura, Hype, Miss 60, Frankie B and Mac & Jac.

Hayes Valley	**415-552-4894**
564 Hayes Street	Wed-Thurs 1-6:30
San Francisco 94102	Fri-Sat 12-7, Sun 12-5:30

Cotton Basics

Stacks of cotton everything are piled into this chain of easygoing wear. Clusters of polychromatic T-shirts, short-and long-sleeves, Vs and plenty of pull-on pants, perfect for lounging around, make up the simple collection. Check out Workwear for a more male-dominated assortment.

Noe Valley	**415-550-8646**
1301 Castro Street	Daily 10-7 (Sun 11-6)
San Francisco 94114	

Berkeley	**510-644-1220**
2907 College Avenue	Daily 10-6:30 (Sun 12-5)
Berkeley 94705	

Oakland	**510-653-0383**
5540 College Avenue	Daily 11-6:30 (Sun 12-5)
Oakland 94618	

Courtoué

Lawyers and doctors don classic duds from this upscale two-level boutique featuring power brands (Brioni, Canali, Versace and Zegna) and an astounding selection of ties. But longstanding clients know Walton Fong's 35-year-old family-run fashion house is also the place for custom-tailored suits and thousands of choices of British and Italian fabrics.

Union Square	**415-775-2900**
459-465 Geary Street	Mon-Sat 9:30-6
San Francisco 94102	

Couture

To stock up on European sportswear, this small stop is worth a look. Light on character but heavy on Italian merchandise, Couture carries the better ranges from lines like Canali, Luciano Barbera, Zanella, Gianfranco Ferré and Couture's own private label. Also find ties, dress shirts, knitwear, a small selection of shoes and lots of leather, especially for women.

Union Square	**415-781-6915**
395 Sutter Street	Mon-Sat 10:30-7
San Francisco 94108	(Sunday by appointment)

CP Shades

Cruising for comfortable clothes? Look no further than CP Shades, the handwoven, loose-fitting fashion cut and sewn in the Bay Area. Always neutral and natural (with a splash of brights here and there), and mightily wash-and-wear friendly, the roomy and carefree clothes come at dependable prices and draw a drove of down-to-earth disciples.   www.cpshades.com

Marin   **415-383-3755**
Strawberry Village   Daily 11-7 (Sun 12-6)
Mill Valley 94941

Cris

Peek at the chic window displays of this Russian Hill spot and you won't believe it's a consignment space. Bargain chasers rely on Cris Zander's picks of old Prada, Armani, Versace, Jil Sander and other once-pricey ready-to-wear faves. Best of all, purchases are packaged in a bag with raffia and fresh flowers—Zander has apparently perfected the art of self-gifting.

Russian Hill   **415-474-1191**
2056 Polk Street   Daily 11-6 (Sun 12-5)
San Francisco 94109

Crossroads Trading Company

Always swarming with secondhand fans, these heavily embraced emporiums scattered across the state are full of up-to-the-minute fashions—used, but in excellent condition. CTC buys, sells and trades your salvageable merch. (Keep in mind, they love the labels). If you're looking for good deals on decent recycled clothes, accessories and shoes, these unassuming outposts are a sure bet.   www.crossroadstrading.com

Castro   **415-626-8989**
2231 Market Street   Mon-Thurs 11-7, Fri-Sat 11-8
San Francisco 94114   Sun 12-7

Pacific Heights   **415-775-8885**
1901 Fillmore Street   (opening times as above)
San Francisco 94115

Haight-Ashbury   **415-355-0555**
1519 Haight Street   (opening times as above)
San Francisco 94117

Oakland   **510-420-1952**
5636 College Avenue   Daily 11-7
Oakland 94618

Crosswalk Specialty Shoes

In a town where practical is more popular than Prada and hills demand to be hoofed, attractive walking shoes have a place in everyone's closet. Enter this new store offering nothing but foot-nurturing fashion since mid-2002. The mostly European collection features Murtosa, chef and doctor favorite Dansko, Merrell, Diesel, earthy-slick slip-on Mephisto options, mules by Born, and the clunky comfort of Wolky.   www.crosswalksf.com

Pacific Heights   **415-921-0292**
2122 Fillmore Street   Mon-Sat 10-7
San Francisco 94115   Sun 11-6

Daljeets

Calling all provocative fetishwear fanatics. Among lots of leather, corsets and a naughty boudoir's worth of clothing for the bordello, Daljeets offers a massive assortment of Doc Marten shoes and boots. Missionites and Haight-walkers come for the many styles of the heavy black cult sole and other clunky and killer heels.

Haight-Ashbury **415-668-8500**
1773 Haight Street Daily 11-8 (Sat 11-7:30)
San Francisco 94117

☆ Dantone

The persistent fashionista knows that despite the merchandising mayhem Farzad Arjmand's corner of floor-to-ceiling chaos is one-stop shopping for tonight's cocktail party. Sexy separates by Vivienne Tam, Miguelina, Cynthia Rowley, Easel, and Big Star snuggle up next to hundreds of handbags, leather jackets, basic black women's suit combos, black boots (stocked year-round) and a steep stack of Europe's slickest shoes. Men stick with the trendy footwear by Alberto Guardiani ("king of Italian shoemakers," declares Arjmand) and Armand Basi duds.

Cow Hollow **415-776-7008**
1796 Union Street Daily 10-7 (Sun 11-6)
San Francisco 94123

Dark Garden

Custom-made corsets whipped up from owner Autumn Carey-Adamme are what's in store at this purple-fronted place. Baroque and brocade, her wispy waist-crunchers are devoured by bust-popping devotees who love the romantic notion of a simple cincher or the bad-girl grit of a tarty leather number. Also find vintage slips, lingerie and wedding garments. www.darkgarden.com

Hayes Valley **415-431-7684**
321 Linden Street Mon-Sat 12-6 (Thurs 12-7)
San Francisco 94102

David Stephen

This oldie but goodie still delivers all the hand-tailored classics it's been dishing out since 1969. Find top-tiered suits and sportswear from a mostly Italian rack of designers—Ermenegildo Zegna, Canali, Vestimenta, Theory. Don't be turned off by its chichi Maiden Lane locale—this unpretentious place pulls in everyone from slick, fashion-friendly tourists to a dapper local set. www.davidstephen.com

Union Square **415-982-1611**
50 Maiden Lane Mon-Sat 9:30-5:30
San Francisco 94108 (Sunday by appointment)

Dean Hutchinson

Canadian createur Dean Hutchinson, who has been on the block since 1992, peddles his unpretentious line on a quiet corner of Presidio Heights. Clean, consistent and not-too-conservative, the collection offers simply cut suits (his signature), pants and separates in fine European fabrics.

Presidio Heights   **415-922-4228**
3401 Sacramento Street   Mon-Sat 11-6
San Francisco 94118   (and by appointment)

Dema

There hasn't exactly been a fashion foray in the newly gentrified Mission district yet, so local designer Dema Grim, who has been cutting her cool collection since 1983, is a big attraction. Shop to the groovy tunes for her geometric silhouettes, packed with a playful sense and punchy prints. Also find Tote Le Monde bags, Three Dots tees and Urchin knits.   www.fabric8.com

Mission   **415-206-0500**
1038 Valencia Street   Daily 11-7 (Sun 12-6)
San Francisco 94110

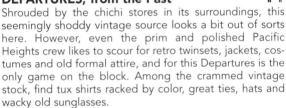

DEPARTURES, from the Past

Shrouded by the chichi stores in its surroundings, this seemingly shoddy vintage source looks a bit out of sorts here. However, even the prim and polished Pacific Heights crew likes to scour for retro twinsets, jackets, costumes and old formal attire, and for this Departures is the only game on the block. Among the crammed vintage stock, find tux shirts racked by color, great ties, hats and wacky old sunglasses.

Pacific Heights   **415-885-3377**
2028 Fillmore Street   Daily 11-7 (Sun 12-6)
San Francisco 94115

The Designer Consigner

Heavy on labels and heaven for the consignment-crazed, this small stop on the Presidio Heights used-clothing circuit stocks all the big boys—from Armani to Calvin and Karl. The mint-condition merchandise (not more than three years old)—shoes, suits, pants and accessories—is never on the rack for more than 60 days. And with Prada prices sometimes more than 70% off, you're sure to be browsing with a bunch of bargain-obsessed babes.

Presidio Heights   **415-440-8664**
3525 Sacramento Street   Daily 10-6 (Sun 11-5)
San Francisco 94118

Designer's Club

This club is not of the haute hype. The Noe Valley boutique is indeed a den of designers, but from the Jessica McClintock, Betsey Johnson and Sue Wong crew. Shirts from Flip, bags by Hype and a jewelry box of dainty baubles also make the everyday mix. Check the back sale rack for bargains.

Noe Valley   **415-648-1057**
3899 24th Street   Mon-Fri 11-6:30, Sat-Sun 11-6
San Francisco 94114

Directory

Dharma

Value victims and cross-cultural fashion fans dig this no-nonsense, patchouli-peppered shop, where printed sari skirts, club-stomping skimpy tops and groovy patterned garb are all served up at budget prices. Ethnic-inspired fashion, beloved in all Dharma's neighborhoods, is what's snapped up, along with scarves, crochet shawls and bags.

Mission 415-920-9855
914 Valencia Street Daily 11-7
San Francisco 94110

Haight-Ashbury 415-621-5597
1600 Haight Street Daily 10-7
San Francisco 94117

Berkeley 510-548-1046
2391 Telegraph Avenue Daily 11-7 (Sun 12-6)
Berkeley 94708

Berkeley 510-548-2282
2116 Vine Street Daily 10-6 (Sun 11-5)
Berkeley 94708

Dialogue

Great for the Pacific Heights guy and gal, this two-for-one shop allows men to get their tennis racket restrung at the Tennis Shack, which resides in the same space, while women browse the collection of Red Engine jeans, Blue Dot and Margaret O'Leary shirts, cord and twill pants, and Weston Wear separates.

Presidio Heights 415-771-4830
3375 Sacramento Street Mon-Fri 10-6
San Francisco 94118 Sat 10-5, Sun 11-5

Dialogue Sport

This sportier sister store across the street carries a more casual assortment of stylish playwear, Om Girl yoga duds and pajamas perfect for the parade of pram-pushing young moms. Don't miss the baby tees and shower gifts too.

Presidio Heights
3376 Sacramento Street Mon-Fri 10-6
San Francisco 94118 Sat 10-5, Sun 11-5

Diana Slavin

Tucked into a funky alley near the financial district is where you'll find this San Francisco-based designer's eponymous collection. Since 1989 Slavin has been dishing out her man-tailored suits, slick knits and easy-going stylish separates, along with an edited assortment of cool ceramics from Ear, jewelry from New York designer Cynthia Lammers, Robert Clergerie shoes and Cutler & Gross shades. www.dianaslavin.com

Union Square 415-677-9939
3 Claude Lane Tues-Fri 11-6, Sat 12-5
San Francisco 94108

☆ Diesel

Ground zero for quintessential street style. The Italian master of youth-culture cool supplies an unabashed mod mix of urban hip to a fashion-courageous crowd. The decidedly Diesel vibe pulses out of the department-store-like digs, where denim is king and cargo is queen, and backpacks, T-shirts, tops and treads all seem to fly out with the crowd.

Union Square   **415-982-7077**
101 Post Street   Mon-Fri 10-8, Sat 10-7, Sun 12-6
San Francisco 94108

☆ Dish

This city has its share of girl-owned boutiques, but Desiree Alexander's Dish was one of the first. Her small, spunky place has plenty on its plate—cool clompers (Cocolico and Woo) and a curvy, cutesy selection of edgy designers for the gals (Juicy, Ulla Johnson, Development, Rebecca Taylor, TKN). www.dishclothes.com

Berkeley   **510-540-4784**
2981 College Avenue   Daily 11-6 (Sun 12-5)
Berkeley 94705

The Disney Store

America's favorite mouse and his friends are mega-merchandised in the retail realm of all things Disney. Shelves of dolls, books, toys and trinkets from the latest animation sensations accompany costumes, nighties, swimsuits and sportswear all geared toward turning your tot into a Sleeping Beauty, Stitch, Lilo, Tinkerbell or Little Mermaid.

Union Square   **415-391-6866**
400 Post Street   Daily 10-8 (Sun 11-6)
San Francisco 94102

Don Sherwood Golf & Tennis World

Bustling with golf and tennis buffs, this massive emporium, which has been swinging since 1964, is the place to satisfy all your fairway and on-court needs. A surefire superstore, Don stocks all the top-of-the-line gear—clubs, balls, shoes, rackets, sneakers and plenty of sportif apparel—to gear up any pro or greenhorn. Be sure to check out the testing tennis tunnel before buying a racket. www.golfandtennisworld.com

Union Square   **415-989-5000**
320 Grant Avenue   Daily 10-6:30 (Sun 11-5)
San Francisco 94108

Dottie Doolittle

The miniature set can make off with a chest full of stylish threads at this long-time neighborhood place, which clothes infants and little girls (up to 14) and boys (up to 8). Snazzy smocked dresses and other fancy fashion hang near baskets stacked with Beanie Babies, ballerina bits and kaleidoscopic frames. There's also plenty of cheery gear from Flapdoodles, Hartstrings and Monkeywear to keep your kids on top of the trends.

Presidio Heights   **415-563-3244**
3680 Sacramento Street   Daily 9:30-6 (Sun 12-5)
San Francisco 94118

Dreamweaver

Betwixt Yoshi and Chanel sits this odd and artsy little boutique, which really has nothing to do with its chichi Maiden Lane neighbors. Dreamweaver shelves a unique inventory of chenilles, nubby knits, crinkly silks and loose-fitting fashions that keeps an art crowd and other eccentric sorts in their unusual offbeat style.

Union Square   **415-981-2040**
171 Maiden Lane   Daily 10-6 (Sun 11-5)
San Francisco 94108

☆ dress

This chic boutique does double duty with two shops—one on each side of the street. At 2271 (the store's original location) Marina babes pop in for a wide range of fashionable casualwear—from the 15 different lines of jeans (including Paper Denim & Cloth, Joie, Seven, Blue Colt, Earl etc.) to trendy tees, yogawear and hip maternity lines from Chaiken, Michael Stars and Diane von Furstenberg. The shop at 2258 focuses on entire collections from designers like Trina Turk and Catherine Malandrino. Owner Yvette Pasco also recently opened the neighboring men's shop, The News, so his & hers couples could divide and conquer.

Marina   **415-440-3737**
2258 & 2271 Chestnut Street   Daily 10:30-6:30 (Sun 12-5)
San Francisco 94123

DSW Shoe Warehouse

Bargain basement believers unite at this warehouse of discount shoes, constantly abuzz with Union Square value hunters. Stripped down and stacked with boxes, this chain features lines like BCBG max azria, Ferragamo, Fendi and bebe, all received weekly and sold at 20-50% off regular department store prices. Don't ask for extra sizes in back—all the inventory is on the floor.   www.dswshoe.com

Union Square   **415-445-9511**
111 Powell Street   Daily 10-9 (Sun 9:30-6)
San Francisco 94102

Duzz 1020

Their business card asks "Do you want to be dazzled?" And the young things who come here are indeed taken with the racks packed with frilly-girl fun. The clingy halters, flowing dresses, fitted slacks and puffy-peasant shirts may be out in six months, but at these prices no one's balking.

Haight-Ashbury   **415-751-7720**
1780 Haight Street   Daily 11-7 (Sunday 11-6:30)
San Francisco 94117

ecco

Fans of functional footwear are who you'll find here. While not always the most fashion-forward, ecco can be counted on for comfort and fit—qualities that keep nature-loving walkers coming back season after season. Find earthy elements in most of their soles, be it Gore-Tex-dipped hiking boots, urban outdoor walkers, plain-toe dress-ups, boat shoes, fisherman sandals or clogs   www.ecco.com

Union Square   **415-956-3461**
236 Post Street   Mon-Fri 10-7
San Francisco 94108   Sat 10-6, Sun 11-6

Eddie Bauer

Affordable fashion for active recreation keeps an outdoor-oriented and casual California set happily clad in EB's outstanding selection of basic tees, tanks, shorts, capris, khakis and swimsuits. Also find footwear and accessories that easily pack into a durable sporty duffle from their travel gear line.   www.eddiebauer.com

Union Square   **415-986-7600**
250 Post Street   Mon-Fri 9:30-8
San Francisco 94108   Sat 9:30-7, Sun 10:30-6

Sunset   **415-664-9262**
Stonestown Galleria   Daily 10-9 (Sun 11-6)
3251 20th Avenue   San Francisco 94132

Peninsula   **650-328-1800**
Stanford Shopping Center   Mon-Fri 10-9, Sat 10-7
Palo Alto 94304   Sun 11-6

☆ emily lee

More mature fashion mavens have come to this Laurel Village haunt to get elegant and artsy chic since Emily Lee, once a buyer for Joseph Magnin, opened her boutique in 1979. Sensibly stylish and loose-fitting staples include Eileen Fisher, Flax, Stephanie Schuster, Joan Vass, Vivienne Tam and French favorite Cop Copine. Tête-toppers by Krista Larson, stretch jeans, Hot Sox and artistic accessories round out the refined but hip modern woman.

Presidio Heights   **415-751-3443**
3509 California Street   Mon-Fri 10-6, Sat 9:30-5:30
San Francisco 94118

Emporio Armani

Giorgio's keen eye for fit and drape is all too apparent at his edgier and sportier offspring. From jackets to jeans, classic pantsuits and black staples, the goods here are for the younger set with an affordable Armani appetite. Best of all is Emporio's café, which offers light and luscious Italian fare, attitude as stiff as the drinks at the bar and sidewalk seating when the weather's right.   www.emporioarmani.com

Union Square   **415-677-9400**
1 Grant Avenue   Daily 11-7 (Sun 12-6)
San Francisco 94108

Enzo Angiolini ⚲

A step up from Nine West's cheap and chic line, Enzo Angiolini places the company's best foot forward. Made up of all the trendy styles of its less sophisticated sibling, this line is just sleeker—beaded sandals, eclectic thongs and sexy, strappy heels.

Union Square   415-512-7081
San Francisco Shopping Centre   Daily 9:30-8 (Sun 10-6)
865 Market Street   San Francisco 94103

Sunset   415-759-9668
Stonestown Galleria   Daily 10-9 (Sun 11-6)
3251 20th Avenue   San Francisco 94132

Financial District   415-986-2866
1 Embarcadero Center   Mon-Fri 10-7, Sat 10-6
San Francisco 94111   Sun 12-5

☆ Erica Tanov ⚲⚲

Boho babes who wish for wispy slips, paper-thin silks and lingerie-like organzas have local designer Erica Tanov on their to-buy list. The diminutive Erica, whose fondness for flea-market finds and vintage lingerie is evident in her women's ready-to-wear and bloomers-and-frock-filled kids' collections, sells an entire world of artistic style in this chic Berkeley boutique. Balancing her lines are Rogan Denim and John Smedley knitwear, Vanessa Bruno tees, Erica Tanov linens and Rosanne Pugliese, Melissa Joy Manning or Beth Orduña jewelry. Tanov also has a store in New York's NoLiTa.   www.ericatanov.com

Berkeley   510-849-3331
1827 4th Street   Daily 10-6 (Sun 11-6)
Berkeley 94710

Erin Paige ⚲

Decently priced duds with a definitive sense of style are sold here. The store itself is nothing to write home about, but with lines like Red Engine, Michael Stars and Eileen Fisher you really can't go wrong. Browse through a sundry of knock-off names like ABS, Max Studio and Tessuto. Easy, no-fuss fashion.   www.erinpaige.com

Cow Hollow   415-885-5362
1849 Union Street   Mon-Wed, Sat 10-7, Thurs-Fri 11-8
San Francisco 94123   Sun 11-7

Escada ⚲

Bedazzling and beaded evening gowns are some of the glitzy gems for which this German house is known. Mothers-of-the-bride, along with the SF social set, hit this two-story shop for its huge assortment of entrance-making merchandise. Also find cocktail suits, plenty of rhinestones and sophisticated sportswear in opulent fabrics, bold hues and racy details.   www.escada.com

Union Square   415-391-3500
259 Post Street   Daily 10-6 (Sun 12-5)
San Francisco 94108

Express

When the clerks have to communicate with headsets you know they're moving a lot of merchandise. And at this chain of low-priced basics and up-to-the-minute styles, which falls under The Limited umbrella, young, cheap thrill-seekers are snapping up all its fad-wear and closet essentials. Find jeans, lingerie, swimwear and every top imaginable in this bustling boutique.   www.expressfashion.com

Union Square   **415-284-9448**
San Francisco Shopping Centre   Daily 9:30-8 (Sun 11-6)
865 Market Street   San Francisco 94103

Sunset   **415-731-1403**
Stonestown Galleria   Daily 10-9 (Sun 12-6)
3251 20th Avenue   San Francisco 94132

Berkeley   **510-848-5030**
2576 Bancroft Way   Mon-Fri 10-7:30, Sat 10-7, Sun 11-6
Berkeley 94704

Marin   **415-927-1499**
Village at Corte Madera   Mon-Fri 10-9, Sat 10-7:30
1520 Redwood Highway   Sun 11-6
Corte Madera 94925

Fenzi Uomo

The refined European-style man is made within the tranquil walls of this small boutique featuring Italian contemporary classics. Well organized and displayed by seasoned professionals, the array here sticks with sure things such as Zanetti suits and casuals, Cavalli jackets, Giorgio Danieli separates and Tulliano silk shirts. Canadian counterparts, such as Jack Lipson shirts and Keith More slacks, and a safe selection of ties add to the allure.

Cow Hollow   **415-563-9700**
1801 Union Street   Daily 11-6 (Sun 2-5)
San Francisco 94123

☆ Fetish

Footwear fetishists beware: this happening habitat of sleek stilettos and precious pumps (think Jane Brown, Christian Louboutin, Sigerson Morrison and Alberta Ferretti) is sure to pump up your passion. The pretty-in-pastels outpost, from Andrea Schnitzer and fashion authority Caroline Heafey, has Pacific Heights princesses prancing in season after season in search of stylish slippers. Also, find à la mode purses, hats and the latest in jewelry. Don't miss Schnitzer's solo endeavor The Bar, the neighboring nook with all that's needed for the glamorous-garment look.

Presidio Heights   **415-409-7429**
344 Presidio Avenue   Daily 10-6 (Sun 12-5)
San Francisco 94115

Fife

There may not be a whole lot of merchandise hanging in designer Andrew Linton's cheery and airy Fife, but it's quality, not quantity, that counts here. In the back of this decidedly hip shop full of house music, Linton cuts a mean black boot-pant, navy fitted duster and super-sexy single-button blouse. Also find a few raw-edged skirts that sling low and luscious.

North Beach   **415-677-9744**
1450 Grant Avenue   Daily 11-7 (Sun 12-6)
San Francisco 94133

fil à fil

For more than a century, these fine French shirtmakers have been serving up wonderfully crafted classics—men's button-downs, women's blouses, smooth backs, short sleeves with pockets—in refined fabrics from traditional pinstripes to a plethora of prints and solids. Folded and hung vertically from their shoulders, the shirts in this small stylized store look as if they popped right off the page of a quality catalog.

Union Square   **415-392-1150**
Crocker Galleria   Mon-Fri 10-6, Sat 10-5
50 Post Street   San Francisco 94104

Fitelle

Favored by youthful working girls who love kicky French fashion. Skinny suits and cutting-edge careerwear that takes you from the bureau to the bars is what's in store here, a fast dose of trusty and trendy style at reasonable prices—belted minis, cashmere sweaters, printed blouses and polished tops.

Union Square   **415-543-8212**
San Francisco Shopping Centre   Mon-Sat 9:30-8
865 Market Street   Sun 10-6
San Francisco 94103

Fleet Feet Sports

Nearby, Marina Green is always rocking with runners, ball-handlers and other bayside sportifs. No foot-fault for Mitchell Masia, the sneaker go-to guy in the Marina. He's been fitting both athletes and non- since 1976 with running shoes and apparel from favorites like Adidas, Nike, New Balance, Brooks, Asics, Mizuno and Sugoi.

Marina   **415-921-7188**
2076 Chestnut Street   Mon-Fri 10-7, Sat 12-6
San Francisco 94123   Sun 11-5

Flight 001

Jetsetters fly in and out of this space-shuttle-like showroom for tomorrow's travel accessories today. The sister shop to the New York flagship opened in March 2002 with space-age stock of sleek luggage, "security friendly" manicure sets, and other mid-air must-haves. Check out their Joy & Jake patent-leather carry-on cases, which hark the high-flying days when stewardesses sashayed down the aisles in boots and mini-skirts.   www.flight001.com

Hayes Valley **415-487-1001**
525 Hayes Street Daily 11-7 (Sun 11-6)
San Francisco 94102

Fog City Leather

More than 30 years of leather know-how makes this small skin-heavy store a reasonable stop. If you're in the market for leather anything—bombers, belts, knapsacks, gloves or caps—stop in. It's worth a look, if only to check out the leather-cutting pros crafting the wares in back. www.fogcityleather.com

Cow Hollow **415-567-1996**
2060 Union Street Tues-Sat 11-6, Sun 12-5
San Francisco 94123

Foot Locker

From this universe of athletic footwear, accessories and apparel family sports fans can find all their favorite styles, brands and sizes. Whether you like to run, play tennis, football, soccer or just walk, Foot Locker is a reliable source for labels from Fila, Adidas and Asics to Champion, Nike, Reebok and Converse. www.footlocker.com

Union Square **415-227-4834**
San Francisco Shopping Centre Daily 9:30-8 (Sun 11-6)
865 Market Street San Francisco 94103

Sunset **415-564-3290**
Stonestown Galleria Daily 10-9 (Sun 11-6)
3251 20th Avenue San Francisco 94132

Mission **415-285-3111**
2829 Mission Street Daily 10-7 (Sun 11-6)
San Francisco 94110

Marin **415-924-5877**
Village at Corte Madera Mon-Fri 10-9, Sat 10-7:30
1814 Redwood Highway Sun 11-6
Corte Madera 94925

Peninsula **650-857-1065**
3225 El Camino Real Mon-Fri 10-8, Sat 10-6, Sun 11-6
Palo Alto 94306

Peninsula **650-326-5919**
320 University Avenue Mon-Fri 10-7, Sat 10-6, Sun 11-5
Palo Alto 94301

Oakland **510-639-7020**
1 Eastmont Mall Mon-Sat 10-7
Oakland 94605

Oakland **510-893-7030**
3275 Lakeshore Avenue Mon-Fri 10-7, Sat-Sun 10-6
Oakland 94610

Berkeley **510-540-4867**
2307 Telegraph Avenue Daily 10-7 (Sun 11-6)
Berkeley 94704

Fossil

You know the company from its funky, priced-within-reason watches. But you may not be familiar with its baggy, boot

45

and carpenter jeans, baseball T-shirts, watches and wallets, all sold in this superstore. Add this brand to the Abercrombie & Fitch and J. Crew crowds' fashion uniform roster.   www.fossil.com

Union Square   **415-296-8630**
55 Stockton Street   Daily 10-8 (Sun 10-6)
San Francisco 94108

French Connection

A fashionable alternative to Banana Republic, this British company hawks affordable, just trendy enough looks watered down from the runways. A reliable source for those who like their style simple, FC has all the slim pants, sunny sundresses and cheerful knits the casual set may desire.   www.frenchconnection.com

Union Square   **415-677-4317**
101 Powell Street   Daily 10-9 (Sun 10-8)
San Francisco 95108

Frette

In late 2000 the Italian master of luxe linen brought its beauteous bed linens, blankets and cozy-chic women's ready-to-wear collection to Union Square. Peek past the seduction of superior sheets for sublime sleep and loungewear in cotton, silk or linen. Little angels can have designer dreams with children's pajamas and robes.   www.frette.com

Union Square   **415-981-9504**
124 Geary Street   Mon-Sat 10-6
San Francisco 94108

Gap

Garbing the dot-com crowd was a simple task for the ubiquitous back-to-basics giant, which is headquartered right here in San Francisco. Even after the dot-bomb, it's still the dependable must-stop for budget-happy staples for just about everyone, serving up khakis, jeans, underwear, T-shirts and a sassy collection of seasonal trends.   www.gap.com.

Union Square   **415-788-5909**
890 Market Street   Daily 9:30-9 (Sun 10-7)
San Francisco 94102

Union Square   **415-989-1266**
100 Post Street   Daily 9:30-8 (Sun 11-7)
San Francisco 94108

Mission   **415-861-8442**
1975 Market Street   Daily 10-8 (Sun 11-6)
San Francisco 94103

Marina   **415-929-1744**
2159 Chestnut Street   Daily 10-8 (Sun 11-6)
San Francisco 94123

Potrero Hill   **415-701-9857**
Potrero Center   Daily 9:30-8 (Sun 10:30-6:30)
2300 16th Street   San Francisco 94103

Financial District — **415-391-8826**
3 Embarcadero Center
San Francisco 94111
Mon-Fri 10-7, Sat 10-6
Sun 12-5

Fisherman's Wharf — **415-392-8380**
1 Jefferson Street
San Francisco 94133
Mon-Sat 10-7
Sun 11-7

Haight-Ashbury — **415-431-6336**
1485 Haight Street
San Francisco 94117
Mon-Fri 10-7, Sat 10-8, Sun 11-7
Sun 11-6

Richmond — **415-751-0551**
4228 Geary Boulevard
San Francisco 94118
Mon-Fri 10-8, Sat 10-7

Sunset — **415-564-6523**
Stonestown Galleria
3251 20th Avenue
San Francisco 94132
Daily 10-9 (Sun 11-6)

Marin — **415-924-2181**
Village at Corte Madera
1542 Redwood Highway
Corte Madera 94925
Mon-Fri 10-9, Sat 10-7
Sun 11-6

Berkeley — **510-540-0667**
2310 Telegraph Avenue
Berkeley 94709
Daily 9:30-7 (Sun 10-6)

Peninsula — **650-326-3668**
Stanford Shopping Center
Palo Alto 94304
Mon-Fri 9:30-9, Sat 10-8
Sun 10-7

Gap Kids & Baby Gap

This ubiquitous chain for newborns to 13-year-olds is virtually unparalleled in the cosmos of cool kids' clothing. It all comes cheap and cheerful in irresistible styles and flavors for fashion-conscious tots and early teens. Be it back-to-school trendiness or about-to-be born gifts, these stores are a sure bet. www.babygap.com

Presidio Heights — **415-386-7517**
3491 California Street
San Francisco 94118
Mon-Fri 9:30-7, Sat 10-7
Sun 11-5

Union Square — **415-788-5909**
890 Market Street
San Francisco 94102
Daily 9:30-9 (Sun 10-7)

Union Square — **415-989-1266**
100 Post Street
San Francisco 94108
Daily 9:30-8 (Sun 11-7)

Potrero Hill — **415-701-9857**
Potrero Center
2300 16th Street
Daily 9:30-8 (Sun 10:30-6:30)
San Francisco 94103

Marina — **415-929-1744**
2159 Chestnut Street
San Francisco 94123
Daily 10-8 (Sun 11-6)

Financial District — **415-421-5266**
(Baby Gap only, not Gap Kids)
3 Embarcadero Center
San Francisco 94111
Mon-Fri 10-7, Sat 10-6
Sun 12-5

Fisherman's Wharf   **415-392-8380**
1 Jefferson Street   Mon-Sat 10-7
San Francisco 94133   Sun 11-7

Sunset   **415-564-7137**
Stonestown Galleria   Daily 10-9 (Sun 11-6)
3251 20th Avenue   San Francisco 94132

Marin   **415-924-4079 (Baby Gap)**
Village at Corte Madera   **415-924-2265 (Gap Kids)**
1542 Redwood Highway Daily 10-9, Sat 10-7, Sun 11-6
Corte Madera 94925

Peninsula   **650-321-5739**
Stanford Shopping Center Mon-Fri 9:30-9, Sat 10-8
Palo Alto 94304   Sun 10-7

GapBody 👨👩

Gap-loving loungers were thrilled when the GapBody concept arrived in the Marina. Find all the cheap and hip pj pants, camis, robes, slippers, tanks, bras, boxers and briefs to under- and outer-outfit any easy-going guys or dolls. It sure makes Sunday strolling in sweats a most acceptable affair.

Marina   **415-447-3986**
2040 Chestnut Street   Daily 10-8 (Sun 11-6)
San Francisco 94123

Union Square   **415-788-5909**
890 Market Street   Daily 9:30-9 (Sun 10-7)
San Francisco 94102

Marin   **415-924-2181**
Village at Corte Madera Mon-Fri 10-9, Sat 10-7
1542 Redwood Highway   Sun 11-6
Corte Madera 94925

Gene Hiller 👨

Sausalito's salute to European menswear runs a grand gamut within its beautiful two-level storefront. Everything the sporting man could want—from ties to tuxes, cufflinks to coats—is here, with known names like Brioni, Canali, Zegna, Pal Zileri and Zanella. Perks include in-house appointments, personal shoppers and tailors.   www.genehiller.com

Marin   **415-332-3636**
729 Bridgeway   Daily 10-6 (Sun 11-6)
Sausalito 94965

Georgiou 👩

San Francisco-based George Georgiou turned one small shop in 1974 into a 60-plus-shop operation selling all his Cyprus-made goods. The stores themselves are still stuck in the Seventies, but the clothes are consummate working-girl garb—suits, trousers, blouses—with enough snakeskin-print, sequins and sparkle to send her into a sassy night. Fast-changing fashion—there's a new collection every month—is often print-happy and contemporary. Check out the SoMa store for steals.   www.georgioustudio.com

Cow Hollow
1725 Union Street
San Francisco 94123
415-776-8144
Mon-Fri 10-7, Sat 10-6, Sun 11-6

SoMa (outlet)
925 Bryant Street
San Francisco 94103
415-554-0150
Daily 10-6 (Sun 12-5)

Union Square
152 Geary Street
San Francisco 94108
415-989-8614
Daily 10-7 (Sun 12-5)

Financial District
3 Embarcadero Center
San Francisco 94111
415-981-4845
Mon-Fri 10-7, Sat 10-6, Sun 12-5

Peninsula
Stanford Shopping Center
Palo Alto 94304
650-473-6575
Mon-Fri 10-9, Sat 10-7
Sun 11-6

Marin
579 Bridgeway
Sausalito 94965
415-331-0579
Mon-Thurs, Sun 10-6
Fri-Sat 10-7

Directory

Ghurka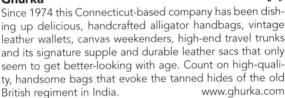

Since 1974 this Connecticut-based company has been dishing up delicious, handcrafted alligator handbags, vintage leather wallets, canvas weekenders, high-end travel trunks and its signature supple and durable leather sacs that only seem to get better-looking with age. Count on high-quality, handsome bags that evoke the tanned hides of the old British regiment in India. www.ghurka.com

Union Square
170 Post Street
San Francisco 94108
415-392-7267
Mon-Sat 10-6

Gianni Versace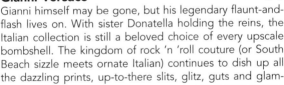

Gianni himself may be gone, but his legendary flaunt-and-flash lives on. With sister Donatella holding the reins, the Italian collection is still a beloved choice of every upscale bombshell. The kingdom of rock 'n 'roll couture (or South Beach sizzle meets ornate Italian) continues to dish up all the dazzling prints, up-to-there slits, glitz, guts and glamour. www.versace.com

Union Square
Crocker Galleria
60 Post Street
415-616-0604
Mon-Fri 10-6, Sat 10-5:30
San Francisco 94104

☆ Gimme Shoes

Fashion hounds whose stamp of style starts from the ground up know that Gimme has the hippest heels this side of the European runways. All the trendy trappings from the likes of Miu Miu, Prada Sport, Dries Van Noten, Demeulemeester, Costume National and Robert Clergerie are stocked at the three outlets around town. More for a black-clad downtown crowd (there's not a Manolo in sight), Gimme feeds those looking for the latest looks in heels, rubber soles and sneakers. www.gimmeshoes.com

Hayes Valley
416 Hayes Street
San Francisco 94102

415-864-0691
Daily 11-7 (Sun 11-6)

Union Square
50 Grant Avenue
San Francisco 94108

415-434-9242
Daily 11-7 (Sun 12-6)

Pacific Heights
2358 Fillmore Street
San Francisco 94115

415-441-3040
Daily 11-7 (Sun 12-6)

Ginger's Bridal Salon

This pink-awning-shaded bridal palace dresses fiancées for success with a wide selection of crafty wedding creations by designers such as Ristarose (which closed its North Beach salon and now shows here), Watters & Watters and Cocoe Voci. Also working for aisle-walking women are sexy shoes (Vera Wang, Richard Tyler, Stuart Weitzman), hair ornaments, veils, handbags and exceedingly tasteful bridesmaids' dresses.   www.gingers-sf.com

Union Square
130 Maiden Lane
San Francisco 94108

415-781-8559
(by appointment)
Wed-Fri 11-7, Tues & Sat 11-6

Gingiss Formal Wear

This formalwear chain serves the time-and-money-crunched man with straightforward service, reasonable prices and a contemporary collection of suits and tuxes by Geoffrey Beene, Ermenegildo Zegna, Oscar de la Renta, Perry Ellis and Chaps Ralph Lauren. Dress-up duds for sale or rent include shoes, vests, studs and cufflinks.

Union Square
170 Sutter Street
San Francisco 94104

415-989-7642
Mon-Thurs 9-6:30
Fri 9-6, Sat 10-5

Sunset
Stonestown Galleria
3251 20th Avenue

415-665-1144
Daily 10-9 (Sun 11-6)
San Francisco 94132

Marin
8950 Northgate Mall
San Rafael 94903

415-491-1100
Daily 10-9 (Sun 11-6)

Giorgio Armani

The taste master's temple to gentle tailoring is an invariably elegant affair, from the tried-and-true suits to the exquisite gowns that can glam up even the most stylishly insecure. If you're looking for flash and pomp, minimalist Armani is not your man. He's a serious style-setter, all about simplicity (something to which his massive celeb clientele can attest) and with an eye for the relaxed and refined, from the accessories right down to the shoes.   www.giorgioarmani.com

Union Square
278 Post Street
San Francisco 94108

415-434-2500
Mon-Sat 10-6

Girl Stuff

Accessory hounds refuel on must-haves-of-the-moment at this girly-girl shop on Polk. Owner Tracy Green-Darian stuffs her tiny pink jewel box with hard-to-find garnishes (at least in San Francisco)—Isabella Fiore bags, Erickson Beamon beads, Janice Savitt jewelry, Hollywood shoes and plenty of trim for your tresses. Pint-size princesses can select from the small but sweet clothing collection.

Nob Hill   **415-409-2426**
2255 Polk Street   Tues-Sat 10-7
San Francisco 94109   Sun 10-5

Girlfriends

Girlfriends Katherine Ribarich and Susan Exposito took their cute and sassy store to Portland a few years back, starting a chain gang of Girlfriends. But this Union Street joint was the gals' first foray into fashion and where they pioneered the adorable Girlfriends logo, splattering it onto T-shirts, tanks and babies' onesies. The rest of the inventory zooms in on a cooler version of the comfy and cozy—Michael Stars, Petit Bateau, Apple Green, Hard Tail—plus plenty of pajamas, perfect for sleepovers. www.girlfriendsboutique.com

Cow Hollow   **415-673-9544**
1824 Union Street   Daily 10-7 (Sun 11-6)
San Francisco 94123

Golden Bear Sportswear

Far less cute and cuddly than the name implies, this longstanding family-owned discount den offers their leather and suede jackets at a fraction of the prices of those sold at Nordstrom and Macy's. Their sporty and sleek styles inspire a variety of bargain-oriented buyers to trek off the usual shopping track to the outskirts of SoMa. www.goldenbearsportswear.com

SoMa   **415-863-6171**
200 Potrero Street   Mon-Thurs 9-5, Fri 9-4
San Francisco 94103

Good Byes

For serious secondhand wear there's nothing quite like the goods at Good Byes. Label fanatics love to forage this pair of shops in well-to-do Presidio Heights in search of big designer names (Armani, Gucci, Donna Karan) pre-owned by the privileged set and listed here at half the retail price. In the summer, casual cuts from Gap and Banana Republic can also be found.

Presidio Heights   **415-346-6388**
3464 Sacramento Street   Mon-Sat 10-6 (Thurs 10-8)
San Francisco 94118   Sun 11-5

Presidio Heights   **415-674-0151**
3483 Sacramento Street   (opening times as above)
San Francisco 94118

Grace Couture

Brides-to-be with more than enough cash to burn might want to schedule an engagement at Grace Couture. This neighborhood place, which outfits many a Pacific Heights princess for her big day, is an Eden of bridal bliss. White wear from Wearkstatt, Reem Acra and Carmela Sutera is lined up, awaiting any well-off blushing bride. Be sure to call for an appointment...walk-ins are not really welcome. www.gracecouture.com

Presidio Heights   **415-771-7875**
3600 Sacramento Street   (by appointment only)
San Francisco 94118

☆ The Grocery Store

Up the street from older sis Susan, where the biz is about the big boys, The Grocery Store serves up less precious and pricey lines with a bit more edge. Homogeneous hipsters in the 'hood hit this fashion emporium for Miuccia's and Yohji's less costly collections (Miu Miu and Y's), Carrie Forbes cashmeres, a fab shoe corner, and funkier labels like Maharishi, Eley Kishimoto, Sold and Fake London.

Presidio Heights   **415-928-3615**
3625 Sacramento Street   Mon-Fri 10:30-6:30
San Francisco 94118   Sat 10:30-6

The Peninsula   **650-348-1372**
311 Primrose Road   Mon-Sat 10-6
Burlingame 94010

Gucci

The fashion world—make that the whole world—turns its head when Tom Ford turns out a new collection. The Gucci guru who single-handedly led the luxury goods house to a fantastically stylish frontier continues to bang out all the glamorous Gucci goodies (shoes, suits, bags, dresses) that keep his insatiable fans wanting more. www.gucci.com

Union Square   **415-392-2808**
200 Stockton Street   Mon-Sat 10-6
San Francisco 94108   Sun 12-5

Guess?

This designer denim pioneer continues to attract attention, and not only for the ad campaigns that sizzle with sex appeal. Teens and cool collegiates can't get enough of the trendy gear—jeans, tight tanks, tube tops, leather looks and denim jackets. The two-story steamy-hot world in Union Square keeps 'em guessing at every turn. www.guess.com

Union Square   **415-781-1589**
90 Grant Avenue   Daily 10-8 (Sun 11-6)
San Francisco 94108

Union Square   **415-495-0200**
San Francisco Shopping Centre Daily 9:30-8 (Sun 11-6)
865 Market Street   San Francisco 94103

Sunset 415-566-3565
Stonestown Galleria Daily 10-9 (Sun 10-6)
3251 20th Avenue San Francisco 94132

Guys & Dolls Vintage

Street strollers sometimes miss Graciela Ronconi's retro outlet, but hep locals know she's got a good stash of Thirties and Fifties vintage duds and accessories, new reproduction shirts by DaVinci and Sun Surf and a few designer finds from stars such as Christian Dior and Hermès.

Noe Valley 415-285-7174
3789 24th Street Mon-Fri 11-7, Sat 11-6, Sun 12-6
San Francisco 94114

Happy Trails

A one-stop pop shop stocked with retro-style housewares, wacky knick-knacks and novelties, this fun-filled place also peddles all manner of fashion whimsy, like fake-fur coats and offbeat separates. Be sure to romp through the magnets, masks and rubber chickens in this newly expanded space. www.shophappytrails.com

Haight-Ashbury 415-431-7232
1615 Haight Street Daily 11-7:30, Fri-Sat 11-8
San Francisco 94117

Harper Greer

Big girls in search of sleek and chic large sizes, look no further than Harper Greer. The SF-based business, which sells its line exclusively here, caters to sizes 14 and up, with a focus on smart careerwear—suits, slacks, blouses and tops— that flatters the larger figure. Count on high-end and high-quality clothing at this roomy shop. www.harpergreer.com

SoMa 415-543-4066
580 4th Street Mon-Sat 10-6, Sun 12-6
San Francisco 94107

☆ Harputs

Sneaker hounds trek to this outer Fillmore outpost, just off the main shopping drag, to find real deals and odd and rare treads. Find Nike and Adidas brought back from the dead, hard-to-find colors and a fab selection of old and unworn athletic footwear. Don't expect a complete range of sizes from the out-of-date inventory, but be sure to check back often to see what's in store. www.harputs.com

Pacific Heights 415-923-9300
1527 Fillmore Street Daily 11-7
San Francisco 94115

Haseena

Fans of the flirty and feminine flock to Rajinder Dua's shop, where reasonably priced frocks from BCBG max azria and Sue Wong sit amongst funky sportswear and run mostly under $100. Find novelty tees, an assortment of jewelry and shoes and lovelies from locals Emily Tees, Weston Wear, and Mary Green's Fifties-inspired bra-and-panty sets.

Hayes Valley
526 Hayes Street
San Francisco 94102

415-252-1104
Sun-Mon 12-6, Tues-Sat 11-7

☆ Heather

Ladies, imagine your most fashionable friend's closet. This purple-and-mint green pad with handcrafted window displays that would give Martha Stewart goose bumps is a small trove of à la mode items. Heather Frazier fills her shop with a revolving roster of hip names—from Mon Petit Oiseau tops and bottoms and Jack Gomme bags to Gauge and John Smedley knits. Style hounds be sure to put this place on your shopping radar, if only for Frazier's picks of new and vintage jewelry.

Pacific Heights
2408 Fillmore Street
San Francisco 94115

415-409-4410
Daily 10:30-6 (Sun 12-5)

☆ Heidi Says

Sisters Heidi and Holly Sabelhaus started a retail website from their Seattle home in 2000, and when business got brisk they opened a store in San Francisco geared toward thirty- and fortysomething gals. The result is this light and airy fashion palace featuring enviable and playful "classics with an edge" from Trina Turk, Rebecca Taylor, Poleci, Nanette Lepore and William B. Drop in with your dog for complimentary biscuits.   www.heidisays.com

Pacific Heights
2426 Fillmore Street
San Francisco 94115

415-749-0655
Daily 11-7 (Sun 11-5)

Held Over

If the massive window displays of kitschy costumes and retro rarities don't pull you in, the inviting, (though to some it may be overwhelming) whiff of incense will. From the owners of La Rosa up the street and other vintage emporiums around town, this almost-creepy goth-like cave keeps the Haight crowd happily clad in old and used duds from the Fifties to the Eighties.

Haight-Ashbury
1543 Haight Street
San Francisco 94117

415-864-0818
Mon-Wed 11-7, Thurs-Sun 11-8

Henry Cotton's

A taste of Tuscany came to SF's main shopping mecca in the form of this 10,000 square foot, five-story space in 2000. Call it modern country, this Italian collection of outdoor-infused sports clothes and ready-to-wear, full of reversible wool and cotton jackets, felted flannel suits and cashmere tops, comes in soothing English-countryside colors…yes, this Italian is promoting Englishness. Find also the hip skiwear line Moncler and dream of schussing the slopes of St. Moritz.   www.henrycotton.co.kr

Union Square
105 Grant Avenue
San Francisco 94108

415-391-5557
Daily 10-6 (Sun 11-5)

Hermès

Find all the luxe leather goods, illustrious silk scarves and ties and, of course, Kelly bags that this posh old maison is still dishing out. Ever since avant-garde Martin Margiela took over the women's design reins, the traditional horsey set has been feeding on a much edgier, yet always elegant, supply of ready-to-wear. Jean Paul Gaultier has joined the team, so watch for even more creative innovations.

Union Square   **415-391-7200**
125 Grant Avenue   Daily 10-6
San Francisco 94108

The Hound

Outfits for the financially savvy who work nearby are what's stocked in this surprisingly spacious store. Mature stockbroker types swing by for the mid-range suits, outerwear, button-down shirts and the casual Hawaiian section in the back. Also find all the accoutrements and accessories to accent the classically dressed man. www.thehound.com

Union Square   **415-989-0429**
140 Sutter Street   Mon-Fri 9:30-6, Sat 10-5:30
San Francisco 94105

House of Blue Jeans

This jeans emporium holds nothing to Levi's high-tech pad up the street but reveals a rocking roster of denim, nonetheless. Tourists love the Guess?, Marithé & François Girbaud and serious Levi's selects, especially since they come at a slightly discounted price. Also find Ecko T-shirts and other urban sportswear. www.americanbluejeans.com

Union Square   **415-252-2929**
979 Market Street   Daily 10-6:30 (Sun 11:30-6)
San Francisco 94103

House of Cashmere

Service may not always be warm and cuddly, but the cashmere classics imported from Scotland and China and sold in this quiet store off bustling Union Street definitely are. Since 1972 this has also been a great stop for wool sweaters and accessories.

Cow Hollow   **415-441-6925**
2674 Octavia Street   Mon-Sat 11:30-4:30
San Francisco 94123

House of Flys

If you aren't down with the dope factor of the Black Flys label, get schooled at this street-chic shop. Techno-rap beats, globe lights and sleek concrete compliment a wall of slick sunglasses and racks of too-cool tees and pants for the fly guy. Girls buzz around the small rack of Black Flys pants.

Haight-Ashbury   **415-621-8122**
1605 Haight Street   Daily 11-7 (Sun 12-6)
San Francisco 94117

Directory

Hoy's Sports

Some say Hoy's is the best running store in the city. Maybe that's because this little shop has been supplying sportifs of the running, racing, track and field type all their sneakers, sweats and technical garb since 1979. Although there's nothing about this gritty neighborhood that welcomes athletes, its proximity to Golden Gate Park is unrivaled. www.hoys.com

Haight-Ashbury   **415-252-5370**
1632 Haight Street   Daily 10-6 (Sun 12-5)
San Francisco 94117

hrm Boutique

This mod Mission shop is the brainchild of the two design-ers whose collections are for sale. Susan Hengst turns out her small women's line of sleek cuts with a dash of idiosyn-cratic details. Her luxe fabrics sit suitably with partner Bob Scales's hrm collection, a modern take on men's style. Revolving art peppers the walls of the clean-cut space and helps keep quietly aesthetic types coming back for more of the understated chic menu.

Mission   **415-642-0841**
924 Valencia Street   Mon, Wed-Thurs 12-7
San Francisco 94110   Fri-Sat 12-8, Sun 12-6

IN-JEAN-IOUS

To clad yourself on Castro Street, the center of gay San Francisco, pop into this general store for all the right gear—cowboy hats, sneaks, jeans, racy racing trunks and sun-glasses. The place has been around since 1991, selling campy Castro-wear and shelves full of T-shirts with tarty, smarty sayings.

Castro   **415-864-1863**
432 Castro Street   Daily 10-9 (Sun 11-7)
San Francisco 94114

ISDA & Co Outlet

In a beautiful turn-of-the-century brick warehouse on Euro-flavored South Park, this West Coast company discounts its Shaker-inspired wares. Media Gulchers gather here on lunch hour, scouring the racks for the pared-down relax-wear (which passes for career clothes in this city), stretchy knits, cozy tees, tweed pants and even silk nightshirts…and all at great prices. www.isda-and-co.com

SoMa   **415-512-1610**
29 South Park   Mon-Fri 10-6, Sat 11-6
San Francisco 94107   Sun 12-5

J.Crew

Those who eschew catalogs for a feel of the real stuff love the basics and city-styling looks in J.Crew stores. Among the affordable tees, tanks, tankinis, rollnecks and sundress-es, find pricier togs in these bricks and mortar venues than on their splashy preppy-life pages, including refined knitwear and slightly dressier outfits. www.jcrew.com

Union Square   **415 546 6262**
San Francisco Shopping Centre   Daily 9:30-8 (Sun 11-6)
865 Market Street   San Francisco 94103

Sunset   **415-731-3901**
Stonestown Galleria   Daily 10-9 (Sun 11-8)
3251 20th Avenue   San Francisco 94132

Peninsula   **650-462-1190**
Stanford Shopping Center   Mon-Fri 10-9, Sat 10-7
Palo Alto 94304   Sun 11-6

Marin   **415-927-2005**
Village at Corte Madera   Mon-Fri 10-9, Sat 10-7:30
1524 Redwood Highway   Sun 11-7:30
Corte Madera 94925

Directory

J.Jill

Followers of this quaint and feminine catalog company were delighted when its sibling J.Jill (the store) opened up. While browsing through the San Francisco Shopping Centre, be sure to peek in for a dose of their easy-going approach to no-nonsense, good-looking fashion. Find everything from ribbed sweaters, knit tops and ribbon-trimmed tees to jersey sweatshirts, washable linen dresses and sandals, shoes and slides.

Union Square   **415-541-9223**
San Francisco Shopping Centre   Daily 9:30-8 (Sun 11-6)
865 Market Street   San Francisco 94103

Marin   **415-924-3933**
Village at Corte Madera   Mon-Fri 10-9, Sat 10-7:30
1546 Redwood Highway   Sun 11-6
Corte Madera 94925

Jaeger

Known for stocking rather conservative wardrobes, this buttoned-up British old-timer is adding some spice to her afternoon-tea look. An overdue update gives the traditional career and sportswear a pinch of punch. Look for slim skirts, zip-front jackets and a safe mix of sweaters and separates, all in fine English threads.

Union Square   **415-421-3714**
272 Post Street   Mon-Sat 9:30-5:30
San Francisco 94108

Japanese Weekend Maternity

Expecting moms, distressed at the thought of shapeless and untrendy clothes, make room in their maternity closet for this hip SF-based designer's duds. Barbie White dishes out fab basics and a menu of innovative patented creations including the Ok™ waistband (an obi-inspired non-restrictive waistband), which comes in cool jeans, shorts, leggings and skirts.   www.japaneseweekend.com

Union Square   **415-989-6667**
500 Sutter Street   Daily 10-6 (Sun 11-5)
San Francisco 94102

Jennifer Croll/Croll Sport

Bridesmaid-pleasing Jennifer Croll has a casual edge, too, evident in the pool table and big-screen TV (though it's hardly ever on). The store has an easy-going vibe, nonetheless, catering to a young Union Street crowd looking for their weekend outfits—jackets, shirts, sundresses, polos and pants from lines like Andrew Marc, Diane von Furstenberg, For Joseph, Tommy Bahama, Ted Baker and Ben Sherman. Also find a bit of bridal and eveningwear.   www.crollsport.com

Cow Hollow   **415-749-1810**
1810 Union Street   Tues-Fri 11-7, Sat, Mon 11-6
San Francisco 94123   Sun 12-5

Peninsula   **408-395-0016**
36 North Santa Cruz Avenue   Tues-Sat 10-5
Los Gatos 95030

☆ Jeremys

Barneys, Bergdorfs and Anthropologie merch, marked down (30-75%) and marketed in a sleek South of Market space. Jeremys is every slave to fashion's fantasy come true—second, end of season, irregulars and customer returns sent in from the top shops. The scene, stocked with designer shoes, bags, gowns and ready-to-wear garments, is tended by sales pros who keep the tempting haute collections in department-store-like order. Cash in at the quarterly sales when the great deals are even greater. You'll know they're happening from the throng out front.

SoMa   **415-882-4929**
2 South Park   Daily 11-6 (Sun 11-5)
San Francisco 94107

Berkeley   **510-849-0701**
2967 College Avenue   Daily 11-6 (Sun 11-5)
Berkeley 94710

Jessica McClintock

Sweet sixteeners, prom-partiers, bridal babes and other formal function-goers have been relying on this romance-maker since 1969. What started as Gunne Sax frou-frou has matured into a McClintock empire encompassing a myriad of lines from fashion to fragrance. Look for dreamy wedding whites, racier dancing duds, strapless pleather numbers, sequins, splash and the super-simple.

Union Square   **415-398-9008**
180 Geary Street, 4th floor   Daily 10-7 (Sun 11-6)
San Francisco 94108

South San Francisco (outlet)   **415-553-8390**
494 Forbes Boulevard   Daily 10-6 (Sun 11-6)
South San Francisco 94080

Jest Jewels

Accessory hounds can't go wrong at these jewelry junked-up shops that feature every kind of extra imaginable. Find anklets, watches, wallets and toe rings or hats, bags and even furry phones. A vast assortment of goods moves in and out of the overwhelming accessorized place, from cheap and trendy to 14-karat gold trinkets.   www.jestjewels.com

Cow Hollow   **415-563-8839**
1869 Union Street   Daily 10-7
San Francisco 94123

Financial District   **415-986-4494**
3 Embarcadero Center   Mon-Fri 10-7, Sat 10-6
San Francisco 94111   Sun 12-5

Berkeley   **510-526-7766**
1791 4th Street   Daily 10-6
Berkeley 94710

Directory

jim-elle

This buttery-yellow neighborhood store doesn't really have a point of view, but take a spin through and you're sure to find some contemporary style among an arty and ethnic-inspired inventory. "Clothes for the fashion confident," says their slogan, meaning a variety of frocks, pants and tops from Lilith, Peter Cohen, Moritz, TSE and Philosophy di Alberta Ferretti.

Pacific Heights   **415-567-9500**
2237 Fillmore Street   Daily 10-6 (Sun 12-6)
San Francisco 94115

Jin Wang

Poofy-ballgown brides don't need to knock on this diminutive designer's door. Jin Wang is all about sleek, chic and refined wedding gear—minimalist with a sophisticated grace that gives elegant Bay Area brides every reason to walk down the aisle. Have a tête-à-tête with Wang, who will sketch and tailor her sheer sheaths and yards of silk to your liking from a selection of samples hanging in her salon.   www.jinwang.net

Union Square   **415-397-9111**
111 Maiden Lane, 3rd floor   Tues-Fri 10-7, Sat 10-6
San Francisco 94108

Joan Gilbert Bridal Collection

Joan Gilbert designed clothes in New York for years before setting up her upscale wedding-dress business in San Francisco. Now she sells most of her refined French and Italian-made gowns, which start at $2,850, through referrals. Brides-to-be stop in her European-style apartment to get fitted and feast their eyes on veils, shoes and jewelry, most of which you won't see elsewhere.

Pacific Heights   **415-752-1808**
San Francisco 94118   (by appointment)

Joanie Char

San Francisco-based designer Joanie Char used to have more shops around town. Now fans of her loose-fitting free-flowing Asian-influenced ensembles flock here for sensational silk robes, eye-catching wraps and linen shirts, jackets and skirt suits preferred by the 40-and-above set. Great prices and a few true finds make it easy to forgive the less luxurious selections.

Union Square	**415-399-9867**
527 Sutter Street	Mon-Sat 10-6
San Francisco 94102	

☆ Joe Pye

Located in the former storefront church of John Coltrane, this store might be a religious experience for the price-conscious fashionista. Owner Juliana Beach stocks the latest looks, with half the items under $100 and the other half under $200. Shoppers go out of their way to hit this destination store between Hayes Valley and the Lower Haight for sweaters from Free People, surf tees from Ashe Francombe, jeans from Citizens for All Humanity and almost anything from Juicy. An added bonus: every few months the store holds a "swap party" for customers to trade clothes.

Haight-Ashbury	**415-355-1051**
351 Divisadero Street	Tues-Fri 12-7
San Francisco 94117	Sat 11-7, Sun 12-5

John Fluevog Shoes

This Vancouver-based designer of the horribly hip boots with big bottoms and bulky toes has clubbers and musicians stomping the Haight 'hood in high style. Fluevogers love the lace-up-to-the-knee boots, heavy-soled cowboy numbers and chunky mules all whimsically cartoon-perfect.

www.fluevog.ca

Haight-Ashbury	**415-436-9784**
1697 Haight Street	Daily 11-7 (Sun 12-6)
San Francisco 94117	

Johnston & Murphy

Suede bucks, woven loafers, cap-toed black oxfords, clogs and earthy sandals are all part of the mix at this 154-year-old company. If this classic shoemaker can't meet your tailored or casual needs with its own designs, it also peddles other labels like Mephisto and ecco. Also find a selection of sportswear, outerwear and accessories. www.johnstonmurphy.com

Union Square	**415-392-0199**
299 Post Street	Daily 10-7 (Sun 11-6)
San Francisco 94108	

Jonathan Kaye Baby

This sprightly store, which looks like the interior of a yellow-hued baby's room, is jammed with delicious kids' stuff from cribs to clothes. Famous for their sturdy wood furniture and baby bedding (see the sibling store across the street), this location offers all the other trimmings for tots and a bounty of babywear (up to 24 months) from companies like Baby Lulu, Zutano, Kushies and Petit Bateau. www.jonathankaye.com

Presidio Heights **415-922-3233**
3615 Sacramento Street Mon-Fri 10-6
San Francisco 94118 Sat 10-5:30

Jorja

Bridesmaids, be sure to keep in mind Jorja on your crusade for wedding clothes. Smack in young and uppity Marina, where wedding-party participants abound, this place is popular for its gown selection from such names as Nicole Miller, Sue Wong, Laundry and Bianca Nero. Accessories are also part of the mix, especially those with a romantic edge.

Marina **415-674-1131**
2015 Chestnut Street Mon-Thurs 11-7
San Francisco 94123 Fri-Sat 11-6, Sun 11-5

The Junior Boot Shop

Presidio Heights parents have relied on this straightforward children's shoe shop since 1937. Whether new foot fashions are meant for a romp (K-Swiss, Nike, New Balance, Teva, Converse, sport socks), stomp (Doc Marten) or to show a little pomp (patent-leather party shoes, ballet and tap shoes, moccasins, tights), more than 60 lines keep little tootsies well tended. Added bonus: the gentle staff and corner of toys soothe impatient kids and their keepers.

Presidio Heights **415-751-5444**
3555 California Street Daily 9:30-6 (Sun 11-5)
San Francisco 94118

☆ Kate Spade

Spade seems to be made for the San Francisco style set. Her ubiquitous bags are toted all around town and gals sport her sandals like walking advertisements. So when this airy white space selling Kate's world of preppy chic— shoes, purses, paper, eyewear and some Jack Spade bags—opened in 2000, handbag junkies were deliriously happy. www.katespade.com

Union Square **415-216-0878**
227 Grant Avenue Daily 10-6 (Sun 12-5)
San Francisco 94108

☆ Kati Koós

Empowering owner Kati Koós says her focus "is on women who have style, not those who want to be in style". Her trove of "timeless but not classic" treasures (Krista Larson, Staley Gretzinger, Giselle Shepatin, Lilith) defies description, although her devout clientele has tried ("urban fairy," "Cindi Lauper grows up," "kooky-chic"). Regardless, fearless fashionistas shouldn't miss her selection, including French baby socks and hand-knit hats tucked in the back.

Union Square **415-362-3437**
500 Sutter Street Mon-Sat 9:30-5:30
San Francisco 94102

Kenneth Cole

Style hounds vehement about value bow down to this all-American shoe guru, who gives feet across the country a fashionable edge. Solid heels and chunky soles, all in the latest trends, makes KC a brand that has an uptown set with downtown attitude slipping into his slides, loafers and lace-ups. Even more affordable and funky are looks from Reaction. Also find a reasonably priced ready-to-wear line and an excellent selection of leather goods.   www.kennethcole.com

Union Square   **415-981-2653**
166 Grant Avenue   Daily 10-8 (Sun 10-6)
San Francisco 94108

Cow Hollow   **415-346-2161**
2078 Union Street   Daily 10-8 (Sun 11-6)
San Francisco 94123

Union Square   **415-227-4536**
San Francisco Shopping Centre   Mon-Sat 9:30-8
865 Market Street   Sun 12-6
San Francisco 94103

Peninsula   **650-853-8365**
Stanford Shopping Center   Mon-Fri 10-9, Sat 10-7
Palo Alto 94304   Sun 11-6

Kids Only

Smack in the middle of this hippy 'hood, it's no wonder this children's shop sells plenty of tiny tie-dye for tykes. Down on the Dead? Not to worry, there's enough offbeat wear, dark duds for baby goths and colorful, handmade playthings for the little ones to keep neighborhood tots crawling and looking cool.

Haight-Ashbury   **415-552-5445**
1608 Haight Street   Mon-Fri 10:30-6:30, Sat 10-6
San Francisco 94117   Sun 11-5

KinderSport

Getting the kids geared up for the Tahoe slopes is a cinch at this winter sport store. It's stuffed to the ceiling with colorful down jackets, sporty skiwear, helmets and other cold-weather paraphernalia from stylish European and American manufacturers like Marker, Spyder, Killy and Couloir. The warmer months are the best time for deals, when most of the store is on sale. KinderSport has shops in the poshest places —Deer Valley, Park City and here in this ritzy neighborhood.   www.kindersport.com

Presidio Heights   **415-563-7778**
3566 Sacramento Street   Mon-Fri 10-6, Sat 10-5
San Francisco 94118

☆ Knitz & Leather

Katharina Ernst and Julia Relinghaus are behind North Beach's longstanding one-two punch of must-purchase sweaters and jackets for femmes of all fashion preferences. Ernst's chunky-chic knits seduce in chenille and mohair while

Relinghaus's fitted leather luxuries wax smart and unique. Locally made glass jewelry and snuggly scarves convince many a city girl to part with more than a few pennies.

North Beach **415-391-3480**
1429 Grant Avenue Daily 11-7 (Sun 12-5)
San Francisco 94133

Kweejibo Clothing Company

Haight Street is a colorful place and individualism is a key characteristic. Maybe that's why Kweejibo has been marketing its men's shirts here since 1995. The double-panel, short-sleeve button-fronts (their signature), and a few styles of basic pants, keep retro-fancying men well fashioned. Best of all, 20% of Kweejibo profits are donated to local and national non-profits. Also find a few women's pieces from SF-based Dema. www.kweejibo.com

Haight-Ashbury **415-552-3555**
1580 Haight Street Daily 11-7
San Francisco 94117

Mission **415-552-3888**
541 Valencia Street Daily 11-7
San Francisco 94110

La Maison de la Bouquetière

Francophiles freak over the profusion of imported housewares, gifts, books, scented laundry products and owner Mario Salas's teas and bath and beauty lines, all of which are packaged to perfection and bagged in Salas's pink answer to Tiffany's trademark blue. Baby gowns and robes from France and Portugal ensure wee ones snooze in style, and sleek slippers give loungers stylishly sure footing. www.labouquetiere.com

Union Square **415-248-1120**
563 Sutter Street Mon-Sat 10:30-7
San Francisco 94102

La Rosa

San Francisco stylists and musicians, fresh from Amoeba Records down the street (one of the city's finest music emporiums), frequent this vintage haunt where high-class clothes from eras gone by (Twenties to Seventies) are plucked for photo shoots and local gigs. In a neighborhood loaded with retro action La Rosa is a quality choice.

Haight-Ashbury **415-668-3744**
1711 Haight Street Daily 11-7
San Francisco 94116

Lady Foot Locker

Girl-power pulsates from this athletic emporium exclusively devoted to women. Find a massive assortment of sports-oriented and fitness footwear, apparel and accessories, from labels like Nike, Reebok, Adidas, New Balance, K-Swiss, Puma and Saucony. Best of all, girls, the salespeople really get it—many are women too. www.ladyfootlocker.com

Union Square	**415-512-9177**
San Francisco Shopping Centre	Daily 9:30-8 (Sun 11-6)
865 Market Street	San Francisco 94103
Peninsula	**650-325-2301**
Stanford Shopping Center	Mon-Fri 10-9, Sat 10-7
Palo Alto 94304	Sun 11-6
Marin	**415-924-5829**
Village at Corte Madera	Mon-Fri 10-9, Sat 10-7:30
1814 Redwood Highway	Sun 11-6
Corte Madera 94925	

Laku

Don't blink or you might miss this tiny gem where Yaeko Yamashita quietly spins her printed and pointy fairytale slippers and all sorts of handmade hats. Look for velvet, silk and linen numbers that she crafts in the back of the store.

Mission	**415-695-1462**
1069 Valencia Street	Tues-Sat 11:30-6:30
San Francisco 94110	Sun 12-5

Lava 9

You'll know you've hit Lava 9 from the fetching waft of freshly cut leather. Here, designer/owner Heidi Werner sells her luscious leather jackets and blazers (sculpted in the back workshop) and a slew of other skins from Identify, A-1 Global Inc and Rem Garson. Cases carrying an enviable collection of chunky silver jewelry with exotic beads are tooled on the premises and hawked among a smattering of other cutting-edge accessories.

Hayes Valley	**415-552-6468**
542 Hayes Street	Daily 12-7 (Sun 12-5)
San Francisco 94102	

Levi Strauss

The SF-bred brand honors its home town with this mega-denim, multi-sensory emporium merging music, art and fashion. The warehousey space, complete with on-line shopping terminals, DJ/VJ booth and listening stations, houses all the classic jeans, engineered and vintage styles plus a corner devoted to fabric ornamentation—beading, patches and appliqués. Be sure to hop in the soaking tub and human dryer with a new pair of shrink-to-fits.   www.levi.com

Union Square	**415-501-0100**
300 Post Street	Daily 10-8 (Sun 11-6)
San Francisco 94108	

Lilith

Find all the whimsical, playful and drapey duds from the fashionable French line at this fanciful North Beach shop designed by SF design duo Fun Display. The colorful collection, cut in everything from linen to tulle in elegant and casual shapes, hangs among a selection of Trippen moccasins and small Il Bisonte leather goods.

North Beach   415-781-6171
1528 Grant Avenue   Sun-Mon 12-5, Tues-Sat 11-6
San Francisco 94133

Lily Samii Collection

During event season (which is nonstop in this socialite-saturated town) the elite fleet like to climb four floors above Union Square to the crisp and clean salon of their local couturier in search of her elegant, hand-spun special-occasion wear. Be it a silk-crepe bias-cut dress or a sleek shift and shimmering jacket, Samii turns out exclusive designs that lunching ladies love.

Union Square   415-445-9505
260 Stockton Street   Mon-Fri 10-6, Sat 10-5
San Francisco 94108

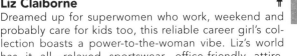

Liz Claiborne

Dreamed up for superwomen who work, weekend and probably care for kids too, this reliable career girl's collection boasts a power-to-the-woman vibe. Liz's world has it all—relaxed sportswear, office-friendly attire, casual basics, shoes, accessories and an extensive petite section.   www.lizclaiborne.com

Financial District   415-788-5041
4 Embarcadero Center   Mon-Fri 10-7, Sat 10-6
San Francisco 94111   Sun 12-5

Loehmann's

You might need some oomph to rake through the racks at this discount clothing emporium. The low-end goods are aplenty, the gems somewhat rarer. Still, if you have the stamina you can get lucky, especially in the famous back room where the more designery duds live (think Donna, Calvin and Giorgio) at bargain prices.   www.Loehmanns.com

Union Square   415-982-3215
222 Sutter Street   Mon-Fri 9-8, Sat 9:30-8
San Francisco 94108   Sun 11-6

Lombardi Sports

Whether you're biking by the bay, hiking in the Headlands, kayaking, in-line skating or surfing at Stinson, Lombardi is the place to gear up. Freshly stocked with the latest athletic equipment from all the big guys (there's a huge Nike selection), this sporty department store has a more extreme, X-Game edge than its competitors. Perfect for the urban sportster.   www.lombardisports.com

Nob Hill   415-771-0600
1600 Jackson Street   Mon-Wed 10-7, Thurs-Fri 10-8
San Francisco 94109   Sat 10-6, Sun 11-6

Lorenzini

This tiny Union Street outpost has been serving up "creative sportswear" to a 20-50-year-old semi-conservative set since 1980. Stocked with mid-fine merchandise, mostly from Italy, Lorenzini (no connection to the Italian collection) peddles everything from jackets to slacks, ties and a few casual suits.

Cow Hollow   415-346-2561
2149 Union Street   Daily 11-6 (Sun 1-5)
San Francisco 94123

Lost Horizon

Tourists won't get lost in Lost Horizon. After all, the place has been offering novelties like wacky sunglasses, T-shirts and fake-fur hats since 1969 to Haight Street habitués. There's not much here for the locals to chomp on, but visitors who want to leave the way-out district with a funky, fashionable souvenir should be sure to stop in.

Haight-Ashbury   415-552-0342
1506 Haight Street   Mon, Tues, Fri 11-5
San Francisco 94117   Wed, Thurs, Sat, Sun 11-6:30

Louis Vuitton

When Marc Jacobs took the driver seat of this venerable leather goods house, he steered its clothing and reputation straight toward hip. Bold enough to splash graffiti on its status logo sacs, edgy enough to monogram trenches and smart enough to carry on the classics, Jacobs has kept the old guard and welcomed a new chic crew.   www.vuitton.com

Union Square   415-391-6200
233 Geary Street   Mon-Sat 10-7
San Francisco 94102   Sun 12-6

Luba

Luba Reeves started selling her designs here decades before the surrounding neighborhood catered to the young café-happy crowd. Now that she and her now-dated style sense have retired to Hawaii, buyer Nellie Kalata is revving up the racy factor with "young contemporary" choices like Cosabella, Juicy Couture, Free People, Bulldog and Mica.

Sunset   415-665-6112
751 Irving Street   Mon-Sat 10-6
San Francisco 94122   Sun 11-5

Lucky Brand

With all-American character, this Los Angeles denim house is stacked with quality goods—literally. Baggy, boot, cargo or chino, low-rise, fit or flare, the pants are piled high, next to bundles of basics—bandana-print pieces, V-tees, cords, shorts and juvenile jeanwear. Lucky dungarees are discernible in the details: the red "Lucky You" on the fly, pocket lining and shirt buttons sporting the cloverleaf logo. If you're in the market for some fine denim, duck your head in this place; you just might get lucky.   www.luckybrandjeans.com

Marina   **415-749-3750**
2301 Chestnut Street   Daily 10-8 (Sun 11-7)
San Francisco 94103

Union Square   **415-281-9020**
San Francisco Shopping Centre   Daily 9:30-8 (Sun 11-6)
865 Market Street   San Francisco 94103

Marin   **415-927-4102**
Village at Corte Madera   Mon-Fri 10-9, Sat 10-7:30
1554 Redwood Highway   Sun 11-6
Corte Madera 94925

Luichiny

Corky mules, chunky-soled sandals, mean motocross boots and platforms that would please even the Pinball Wizard are what this Italian funky footwear collection is all about. Rockers, ravers and anyone who likes a lift go for the young and trendy treads that come at fairly easy prices.   www.luichiny.com

Haight-Ashbury   **415-252-7065**
1529 Haight Street   Daily 11-7 (Sat 11-8)
San Francisco 94117

L'Uomo International

Locals love these small specialty boutiques for their snazzy and slick European (mostly Italian) selections from designers like Vestimenta, Ferragamo, Hugo Boss, Brioni, Zegna and Lorenzini. Find fine suits, leather looks, jeans, sportswear and shoes from Ferragamo, Cole Haan and Zegna—smart tailoring for men from head to toe. www.luomointernational.com

Pacific Heights   **415-776-0669**
2121 Fillmore Street   Daily 11-7 (Sun 11-6)
San Francisco 94115

Peninsula   **408-247-6100**
Stanford Shopping Center   Mon-Fri 10-9, Sat 10-7
Palo Alto 94304   Sun 11-6

MAC

The super-stud fashion school knows that MAC (short for Modern Appealing Clothing) peddles that perfect little Patch bag, A.F. Vandervorst dress, snazzy Timothy Everest tie, Armand Basi suit or Paul Smith accessory they just can't live without. The quirky shops (girls on Grant Avenue, guys on Claude Lane), peppered with vibrant vintage vases and kooky lamps (all for sale), are run by siblings Chris and Ben Ospital who have been bartering their too-cool style for more than 20 years. Bonus: the men's store has a corner dedicated to GEORGE's fashionable doggy duds and Miller et Bertaux deco details.

Union Square (men)   **415-837-0615**
5 Claude Lane   Daily 11-6 (Sun 12:30-5)
San Francisco 94108

North Beach (women)   **415-837-1604**
1543 Grant Avenue   (opening times as above)
San Francisco 94133

Macy's

A major makeover with six-story glass windows makes this massive Macy's at 700,000 square feet one of the largest stores in the world. There are eight floors—including a cheesecake factory and fantastic Bay Area views from the top—of non-intimidating fashion, accessories and house-wares, complete with thousands of pairs of jeans and duds from mid-range designers like DKNY, Tommy Hilfiger and Jones New York.

Union Square
170 O'Farrell Street
San Francisco 94102

415-397-3333
Mon-Wed 10-8, Thurs-Sat 10-9
Sun 11-7

Sunset
Stonestown Galleria
3251 20th Avenue

415-753-4000
Daily 10-9 (Sun 11-7)
San Francisco 94132

Peninsula
Stanford Shopping Center
Palo Alto 94303

650-326-3333
(opening times as above)

Marin
Village at Corte Madera
1400 Redwood Highway

415-927-3333
(opening times as above)
Corte Madera 94925

Maison De Belles Choses

Owner Ellen Fletcher Kelly is in a frenzy for all things French. In this homey shop in a posh neighborhood she hawks everything from provençal pottery to wrought-iron beds and a potpourri of precious children's clothes—cus-tom-made raincoats for kids, smocked dresses with peter pan collars. Francophile moms will love the classic Parisian purses (à la Kelly bag).

Presidio Heights
3263 Sacramento Street
San Francisco 94115

415-345-1797
Daily 10-6 (Sun 11-5)

Manifesto:

In this quirky boutique just off the main Hayes Valley artery, Sarah Franko and Suzanne Castillo display their unique assortment of affordable Forties and Fifties-ish blouses, dresses and pants cut from vintage-inspired fab-rics on a table right in the middle of the shop. Under the sky-blue, cloud-filled ceiling the designing duo also ped-dle retro-looking purses and bits of adorable, offbeat babywear. www.manifestoclothing.com

Hayes Valley
514 Octavia Street
San Francisco 94102

415-431-4778
Tues-Fri 11-7
Sat 10-6, Sun 12-5

☆ Marc Jacobs

The former guru of grunge, now master of cutting-edge conservative chic, opened this store in 2000 to the cheers of San Francisco's style elite. Hipping up a fading Maiden Lane, this sleek space houses all Jacobs's coveted clothes—tweed suits, prim and in pumps, pretty dresses and cashmere sweaters—and his addictive selection of accessories and undertrimmings.   www.marcjacobs.com

Union Square   415-362-6500
125 Maiden Lane   Mon-Sat 10-6 (Thurs 10-7)
San Francisco 94108   Sun 12-5

☆ Margaret O'Leary

O'Leary, a local creatrice born in Ireland who favors layered looks in Lycra, wool and rayon, boasts four eponymous shops in the area. They brim with all sorts of fashionable goodies, including her casually hip line loaded with nubby knits. Dot-commies and chic mommies count on her for Sigerson Morrison steps, Rozae Nichols night dazzlers, a dash of Dosa, Il Bisonte wallets, Paul Smith eyewear and Me & Ro jewelry. Also find a smattering of knitwear for men.   www.margaretoleary.com

Union Square   415-391-1010
One Claude Lane   Tues-Sat 10-5
San Francisco 94108

Pacific Heights   415-771-9982
2400 Fillmore Street   Mon-Sat 10-6
San Francisco 94115

Marin   415-388-2390
14 Miller Avenue   Daily 10-6 (Sun 12-5)
Mill Valley 94941

Berkeley   510-540-8241
1832 4th Street   Daily 10-6 (Sun 11-5)
Berkeley 94710

Marina Morrison

Uptown Bay Area brides, fresh from registering at Gump's, ride the elevator just outside to the fourth floor, where Marina Morrison's stock of upscale princess poofs, sheaths and elegant ivories are to be found. The chic shop peddles the finest in wedding finery—creations from Richard Glasgow, Peter Langner, Ulla-Maija and other unique and precious collections.

Union Square   415-984-9360
30 Maiden Lane   Tues-Sat 10-6 (Thurs 10-7)
San Francisco 94108   (by appointment)

Marmot Mountain Works

Gearheads serious about the great outdoors make the trek to this East Bay emporium for its top-notch tackle. Don't be fooled by its name, this cool camping, mountaineering and backcountry skiing boutique, housed in a converted Russian Orthodox church, is packed not only with high-tech Marmot equipment but also with active and protective apparel from Patagonia, Prana, Arc'teryx and Stonewear Designs.   www.marmotmountain.com

Berkeley   510-849-0735
3049 Adeline Street   Mon, Thurs-Fri 10-8
Berkeley 94703   Tues-Wed, Sat 10-6, Sun 11-5

Mars Mercantile

Berkeley students break away from studies to sort through the vast collection of vintage and thrift at this affordable double-decker destination. The focus is on fashions from the Forties to the Seventies, but a little digging will unearth everything from goth goodies to costume-party classics.　　　　　　　　　　　www.marsmercantile.com

Berkeley　　　　　　　　　　　　　　　　**510-843-6711**
2398 Telegraph Avenue　　　　　Sun-Thurs 11-7, Fri-Sat 11-8
Berkeley 94704

Marshalls

Massive amounts of merchandise from this season (and last?) cram into this discount store. Activewear, sportswear, dress shirts, business casual attire and California-relaxed basics come at 20-60% off regular department and special-ty store prices. A good bet for T-shirts, underwear and sneaks at rock bottom prices.　　　www.marshallsonline.com

Union Square　　　　　　　　　　　　　**415 974-5368**
901 Market Street　　　　　　　　　　　　Daily (Sun 11-8)
San Francisco 94103

Marin　　　　　　　　　　　　　　　　**415-924-3960**
313 Corte Madera Town Center　　　　　Daily 9:30-9:30
Corte Madera 94925　　　　　　　　　　　　(Sun 11-6)

Martha Egan

This offbeat place on the fringe of the financial district and North Beach just might be the quirkiest shop in the city. Egan cuts kooky clothes in vintage patterns (Forties frocks, Fifties button-fronts) and retroesque fabrics, from loud prints to simple solids. Her designs are immediately recog-nizable from the whimsical rectangles that serve as her labels.　　　　　　　　　　　　www.marthaegan.com

North Beach　　　　　　　　　　　　　**415-397-5451**
1 Columbus Avenue　　　　　　　　　　　　Tues-Sat 11-6
San Francisco 94111

MaxMara

Think clean, camel and cashmere—that's the mood of MaxMara's contemporary chic boutique. Italy's stylish staple (there's a shop on just about every corner) boasts a light and airy shop here, as warm and inviting as their winter wools and summer linens. There's hardly a print in sight, only fabulous twinsets, comfortably luxe coats and cash-mere sweaters in cool creamy hues. Sleek leather bags and sunglasses finish off MaxMara's sporty, elegant and oh-so-Italian look.

Union Square　　　　　　　　　　　　**415-981-0900**
175 Post Street　　　　　　　　　　　　　Mon-Sat 10-6
San Francisco 94108

Peninsula　　　　　　　　　　　　　**650-327-1100**
Stanford Shopping Center　　　　　Mon-Fri 10-9, Sat 10-7
Palo Alto 94304　　　　　　　　　　　　　　Sun 11-6

Max Nugus Haute Couture

It's an incognito stop on the haute couture circuit, but San Francisco socialites know to sashay past the neighboring coffee shop swarming with foreign exchange students and into designer Max Nugus's discreet den of fashion decadence. As at his outposts in Beverly Hills and Palm Desert, gowns glimmer (think French lace, embroidery, crystals), shoes shimmer and Nugus promises: "If I can't make you look fabulous, try surgery." Brides also drop in to be done up.

Union Square **415-956-6469**
537 Sutter Street Mon-Sat 10-5
San Francisco 94102 (or by appointment)

The Men's Wearhouse

Guys looking for goods at a good price rely on this one-stop shop for designer duds discounted by an average of 30-40%. Find a slew of suits from leading labels—DKNY, Canali, Hugo Boss and Gianfranco Ferré, for example—and also a lot of schlock. Dress shirts, tuxes, sportswear and even socks are on the menu, in addition to great steals on soles from Cole Haan, Florsheim, Bostonian and more. www.menswearhouse.com

Union Square **415-544-0627**
17 Stockton Street Mon-Fri 10-8, Sat 10-6
San Francisco 94108 Sun 11-6

☆ Metier

Creative professional women (architects, designers and local gallery types) love this elegant shop for work-to-eveningwear with a feminine edge. Owner Sheri Evans features fashion-forward lines like Blumarine, Development and Mayle plus accessories and jewelry. Her collection of vintage and estate jewelry also draws the non-traditional wedding set. www.metiersf.com

Union Square **415-989-5395**
355 Sutter Street Mon-Sat 10-6
San Francisco 94108

MetroSport

Marathoners, joggers and general sneaker-clad sportifs count on this small running-oriented retailer, which stocks one of the best selections of sneaks in the city. Among the Nike, Adidas, Brooks, New Balance, Asics and Saucony styles, find an assortment of triathlon garb—everything from Pearl Izumi biking gear to Speedo suits and Quintana Roo wetsuits.

Cow Hollow **415-923-6453**
2198 Filbert Street Mon-Fri 10-8, Sat 10-6, Sun 10-5
San Francisco 94123

Peninsula **650-321-6453**
37 Town & Country Village Mon-Fri 10-8, Sat 10-6
Palo Alto 94301 Sun 11-6

Directory

Mill Valley Hat Box

Once in San Francisco and now open only in Marin, this top shop is still a mad-hatter smattering of Easter-worthy bonnets, cool caps, crushers and the latest lids. Find Eric Javits creations, Helen Kaminski's sweet numbers and Kangol's hip-hop hats, among a load of straw bags, hair accessories and the foxiest hatboxes around.

Marin   **415-383-2757**
118 Throckmorton Avenue   Daily 10-6 (Sun 12-6)
Mill Valley 94941

Mimi Maternity

Practical and pretty affordable, this maternity mall shop offers a closet full of passably stylish clothes for the nine-month haul. Weed through the plain and simple stuff and hunt down the snazzy summer dresses, sweaters, capris, big tees and bathing suits. Gals depend on their boot-cut, easy-care pants and count on MM for big-girl underwear.   www.mimimaternity.com

Marin   **415-945-3275**
Village at Corte Madera   Mon-Fri 10-9, Sat 10-7:30
1618 Redwood Highway   Sun 11-6
Corte Madera 94925

Minis

On the bottom floor of this grand Victorian building Christina Winchel peddles her cute collection of kids' and maternity wear. Feeding infants up to size 10, the Minis line, which she handcrafts from her garage, is a playful bunch of jumpers, dresses, onesies and tops. Expecting moms can also find comfy maternity clothes and teeny high-end soles for their tots.   www.minis-sf.com

Cow Hollow   **415-567-9537**
2278 Union Street   Daily 10:30-6:30 (Sun 11-5)
San Francisco 94123

Minnie Wilde

Terri Olson and Ann D'Apice, a pair of pixie designers, preside over this tiny blue-mosaic-tiled shop with plastic Gerber daisies dangling from the ceiling. Their vintage-twisted line, Minnie Wilde, is funky and feminine—the cute and cutting-edge dresses, pants and tops boast vintage details like pin-tucking, back pleats and little ties. Find Seventies-inspired disco dresses, modular skirts with snap-changing panels and halters that convert to bikini tops.   www.minniewilde.com

Hayes Valley   **415-863-WILD**
519 Laguna Street   Tues-Sat 12-7, Sun 12-5
San Francisco 94102   (Monday by appointment)

Mio

Architecturally and texturally inspired layers have been Miyo Ota's inspiration since she opened this shop in 1986—"we dress women and not little girls," she says. That means an arty and eclectic selection from lines like Harari, Shirin Guild, Longchamp or Rundholz. There is also a small assortment of hats and bags.

Pacific Heights　　　　　　　　**415-931-5620**
2035 Fillmore Street　　　　　　Daily 10-6 (Sun 12-5)
San Francisco 94115

Mix

You'd be remiss to walk by this discreet little shop, especially if you're in the market for a unique piece of something special. For nearly a decade Mix has been merchandising high-end, one-of-a-kind creations from little-known or offbeat and exotic designers like Annette Gortz, Sophie Hong, Masahiro Miyazaki and Chacok.

Union Square　　　　　　　　**415-392-1742**
309 Sutter Street　　　　　　　　Mon-Sat 10-6
San Francisco 94108

Mom's the Word

Set in a district fertile with moms-to-be, this easy-going shop has enough stretchy and stylish stuff to keep expecting ones contemporary. Wide-cuff denim, big old briefs, nursing gear, stylish suits and even velvet evening clothes are all on the menu. The large, moderately priced selection from lines like Japanese Weekend, Linique and L'Attesa make this place a destination stop on the maternity circuit.　　　www.momstheword.com

Presidio Heights　　　　　　　**415-441-8261**
3385 Sacramento Street　　　　Daily 10-6 (Sun 12-5)
San Francisco 94118

Mona Lisa

Femmes whose favorite buzzwords are sheer, floral, frilly-fun and French drop by this reasonably cheap boutique for a small selection of flamboyant finds in the form of silk dresses, slick slacks and designer denim. Check out the back rack for racy rainproof coats.

Cow Hollow　　　　　　　　　**415-346-8190**
2277 Union Street　　　　　　　Daily 11-7 (Sun 12-5)
San Francisco 94123

Mrs Dewson's Hats

Fabulously outspoken Mrs Dewson has been at the head of this unassuming and overwhelmingly stocked hat shop in posh Pacific Heights for more than a quarter of a century. Peek past the pics of her happy customers to find Kangol, Borsalino and Stetson among other classic cloches, berets and floral and feather frou-frou. The "Willie Brim," a fur felt snap-brim fedora, is one of many of her own designs—this one created for the hat-loving mayor, Willie Brown.　　　　　　www.mrsdewsonhats.com

Pacific Heights　　　　　　　**415-346-1600**
2050 Fillmore Street　　　　　Tues-Sat 11-6, Sun 12-4
San Francisco 94115　　　　　　(and by appointment)

Directory

☆ Mudpie

Everything for the well-heeled little prince and princess, including pint-size polished looks and an air of European flair. This charming but pricey Cow Hollow place is a magnet for upscale mommies who like to fuss over their privileged kid's fashion. They find mini three-piece suits, cushy fleece, delicate dresses and satin kimonos, as well as tables of toys and accessories.

Cow Hollow　　　　　　　　　**415-771-9262**
1694 Union Street　　　　　　　Daily 10-6 (Sun 11-5)
San Francisco 94123

My Boudoir

Owner Gerri Donato buys a fab blend of haute-designer and low-fuss lingerie for her purple, lilac and gold boudoir. The flirty undertrimmings come from International lines like Simone Perele, Parah, Aubade, Eda, Chiarugi and Cosabella. Also find a small selection of ready-to-wear treats from Beautiful People and Tracy Reese under which your naughty-and-niceties can go.　www.myboudoir.net

Pacific Heights　　　　　　　**415-346-1502**
2029 Fillmore Street　　　　　Mon-Fri 11-7, Sat 10-7
San Francisco 94115　　　　　　　　　　　Sun 11-6

Neiman Marcus

San Francisco's grande dame of department stores flaunts its Texas roots in this opulent store with its Philip Johnson-designed front. Cases of glitzy costume jewelry under a great glass atrium greet SF's fashion elite, who come to hunt for heels in one of the best shoe departments in town and to seek out the chicest names in the fashion universe. For the past two years the six-floor store has been getting a major makeover, inside and out. By 2004 we can expect a new Geary Street entrance, a sidewalk café and more store footage, to make it the biggest NM in the country.　　　　　　www.neimanmarcus.com

Union Square　　　　　　　　**415-362-3900**
150 Stockton Street　　　Mon-Sat 10-7 (Thurs 10-8)
San Francisco 94108　　　　　　　　　　　Sun 12-6

Peninsula　　　　　　　　　　**650-329-3300**
Stanford Shopping Center　　　Mon-Fri 10-8, Sat 10-7
Palo Alto 94304　　　　　　　　　　　　　Sun 12-6

New Balance

What started as an orthopedic shoe and arch support business almost a century ago has blown into an entire athletic footwear universe. Known for their form and fit, these sneaks come in a wild assortment of sizes and widths, durably made for anyone from elite athletes to weekend warriors. Also find NB's line of water-resistant, breathable, microfibered and general high-tech sports apparel.　www.newbalance.com

Union Square　　　　　　　　**415-788-6273**
222 Sutter Street　　　　　　　Mon-Fri 10-8, Sat 10-6
San Francisco 94108　　　　　　　　　　　Sun 11-5

The News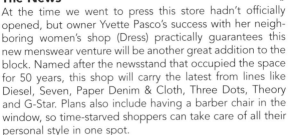

At the time we went to press this store hadn't officially opened, but owner Yvette Pasco's success with her neighboring women's shop (Dress) practically guarantees this new menswear venture will be another great addition to the block. Named after the newsstand that occupied the space for 50 years, this shop will carry the latest from lines like Diesel, Seven, Paper Denim & Cloth, Three Dots, Theory and G-Star. Plans also include having a barber chair in the window, so time-starved shoppers can take care of all their personal style in one spot.

Marina   **n/a at press time**
2260 Chestnut Street
San Francisco 94123

☆ Nida

Finely focused on the Italian fashion fleet, this small space is a dream find for men and women pining for the best in Prada Sport, Miu Miu and Costume National. Not Italian, but a favorite among fashionistas, Helmut Lang is also available. The well-chosen selection includes shoes, sweaters, skirts and a fab spread of outerwear. It's one of the only high-fashion stops on store-crammed Union Street, so be sure to fill your Prada pouch with plenty of cash.

Cow Hollow   **415-928-4670**
2163 Union Street   Daily 11-7 (Sun 12-6)
San Francisco 94123

Hayes Valley   **415-552-4670**
544 Hayes Street   (opening times as above)
San Francisco 94102

Niketown

The monster of marketing machines beckons fans of the swoosh to this high-tech athletic lab, complete with video screens and Jetsonesque sneaker-transporting tubes. Fashionable sports fans and teams of teens flood this place for the latest treads, trunners, cages, watches and high-tech performance duds.   www.nike.com

Union Square   **415-392-6453**
278 Post Street   Daily 10-8 (Sun 11-7)
San Francisco 94108

Nine West

These saucy soles may not last more than a season or two, but who cares—they don't make a dent in your bank account. The dirt-cheap mod moccasins, mules and plumped-up pumps, and even the trendy trench coats, matte jersey dresses, printed slips and floral clutches feed a bubble-gum culture that snaps up the trendy wares by the second.   www.ninewest.com

Cow Hollow   **415-929-0829**
2086 Union Street   Daily 10-8 (Sun 11-6)
San Francisco 94123

Directory

Union Square	**415-243-8850**
San Francisco Shopping Centre	Daily 9:30-8 (Sun 11-6)
865 Market Street	San Francisco 94103
Union Square	**415-772-1924**
250 Stockton Street	Daily 10-7 (Sun 11-6)
San Francisco 94108	
Financial District	**415-986-4592**
4 Embarcadero Center	Mon-Fri 10-7, Sat 10-6
San Francisco 94111	Sun 12-5
Sunset	**415-731-0119**
Stonestown Galleria	Daily 10-9 (Sun 11-6)
3251 20th Avenue	San Francisco 94132
Peninsula	**650-473-9607**
Stanford Shopping Center	Mon-Fri 10-9, Sat 10-7
Palo Alto 94304	Sun 11-6
Marin	**415-924-5910**
Village at Corte Madera	Mon-Fri 10-9, Sat 10-7:30
1724 Redwood Highway	Sun 11-6
Corte Madera 94925	

Net-a-Porter

You won't find this shop on any high street—it's London's best virtual boutique, created by a gang of brilliant alumnae from that stylish and unique magazine *Tatler*. The original concept was to create an online magazine with fashion features just like the glossies, but which visitors could buy from (see Gisele in a stunning Missoni bikini, double-click and it's yours). The idea has since expanded into an online emporium of hot designer names, featuring gypsy tops by Marc Jacobs, Maharishi cargo pants, Jeans by Seven, and Cacharel eveningwear. Shoes by luminaries like Christian Louboutin and Jimmy Choo, and separate sections for beauty, jewelry and music, make this a chic one-stop shop for those who prefer logging on to trekking about.   www.net-a-porter.com

☆ Nomads

Ground zero for the hip and happening guy, Nomads serves up a menu of mod, fresh and edgy fashion. "Not disposable," says owner Keyvan Behnia who favors classic cool lines like Oliver Spencer, Coast, Hermanos, Esteban Cortezar, Von Dutch, G-Star, and Nixon watches. Aside from the funky threads, check in with Behnia, who doubles as a DJ at Dalva in the Mission, to tune into what's groovin' on the SF night circuit.

Hayes Valley	**415-864-5692**
556 Hayes Street	Sun-Mon 11-6, Tues-Sat 11-7
San Francisco 94102	

Nordstrom

Known for its exceptional customer service (they'll take back almost anything), this family-run department store whose Seattle roots were in shoes has grown into a 126-store chain serving up fine jewelry, shoes, cosmetics and a user-friendly medley of high and low fashion. Don't miss the Spa at Nordstrom (Union Square)—it's hands down one of the best escapes in the city.   www.nordstrom.com

Union Square   **415-243-8500**
San Francisco Shopping Centre   Daily 9:30-9 (Sun 10-7)
865 Market Street   San Francisco 94103

Sunset   **415-753-1344**
Stonestown Galleria   Mon-Sat 10-9
285 Winston Drive   Sun 11-7
San Francisco 94132

Marin   **415-927-1690**
Village at Corte Madera   Mon-Fri 10-9, Sat 9:30-8
1870 Redwood Highway   Sun 10:45-7
Corte Madera 94925

Peninsula   **650-323-5111**
Stanford Shopping Center   Mon-Fri 10-9, Sat 10-8
Palo Alto 94304   Sun 11-7

Directory

North Beach Leather 👤👤

This San Francisco constant is the first stop on any leather-lover's list. It has been doling out its snazzy hides since 1967 and has garbed every Seventies musician and hippy imaginable. In 1998 it opened this flagship store to house all its chestnut, chocolate, black and rainbow-rich leathers—boot-cut or hip-hugging pants, jackets, jumpsuits, blazers, skirts and dresses. Although the simple stuff is always in stock, NBL is a fan of slickster embellishments: watch for embroidery, sequins, beading and stitching.   www.northbeachleather.com

Union Square   **415-362-8300**
224 Grant Avenue   Daily 10-7 (Sun 12-6)
San Francisco 94108

The North Face 👤👤👤

Gearheads who bag fourteeners like a walk in the park, or find avalanche conditions arousing, outfit at this rugged outdoor-equipment maker for all their off-the-wall adventures. Tents, jackets, fleece, under and outerwear in high-tech textiles and high price tags are just a sample of what's in store, along with a bevy of backpacks, day packs and durable duffles.

Union Square   **415-433-3223**
180 Post Street   Daily 10-8 (Sun 11-6)
San Francisco 94108

Peninsula   **650-327-1563**
217 Alma Street   Mon-Fri 10-8, Sat 10-6, Sun 11-6
Palo Alto 94301

Berkeley (outlet)   **510-526-3530**
1238 5th Street   Daily 10-7 (Sun 11-5)
Berkeley 94701

Ocean Front Walkers 👤👤

This quirky, slim shop has a simple philosophy: Hawaiian shirts and cozy sleepwear. Lining the walls are racks of

Avanti's retro-style silk aloha button-fronts, P.J. Salvage jammies, Nick & Nora robes, plenty of loungewear and a bundle of bright boxer shorts.

Noe Valley   **415-550-1980**
4069 24th Street   Daily 11-6 (Sun 12-5)
San Francisco 94114

☆ Oceana Rain

Another girly shop for the Pacific Heights pedicured set that counts on the discerning eye of owner Oceana Rain Stuart. Blending all the right ingredients to please her posse of young and trendy fans, Stuart's smart line-up of items-of-the-moment includes refreshing faves like Shoshanna, Diane von Furstenberg, Catherine Malandrino, Tracy Reese, Sage jewels and European shoes. Also find the essential lingerie and loungewear to underlayer all the goodies.   www.oceanarain.com

Cow Hollow   **415-346-2797**
3024 Fillmore Street   Mon-Fri 10-8, Sat 10-7
San Francisco 94123   Sun 10-6

Oilily

Toddlers in Technicolor love the kooky cuts from this Dutch design duo. Floral-printed frocks, plaids, polka dots, striped sweaters, tops with talking animals and plenty of juicy-fruit hues make up this fun-filled collection for kids, girls and even their color-crazed moms.   www.oililyusa.com

Peninsula   **650-323-1996**
186 Stanford Shopping Center   Mon-Fri 10-9, Sat 10-7
Palo Alto 94304   Sun 11-6

Old Navy

Hasn't Morgan Fairchild said it all? Dirt-cheap basics that even the super-stylish can't resist are stocked at these warehousey shops from the Gap family tree. Pick up cotton T-shirts, sweats, swim trunks, jackets and jeans and be set to send them straight to the Salvation Army by next season.   www.oldnavy.com

Union Square   **415-344-0376**
801 Market Street   Daily 9:30-9 (Sun 11-8)
San Francisco 94103

Potrero Hill   **415-255-6814**
Potrero Center   Daily 9:30-8 (Sun 10:30-6)
2300 16th Street   San Francisco 94103

Old Vogue

When local swing kids want to get swank they stop in this straightforward vintage shop known for housing the city's best collection of smoking jackets. Since 1985 retro revelers have been ransacking the racks for yesterday's Burberry coats, cashmere sweaters, Levi jackets, 501 jeans, Hawaiian shirts and groovy getups by Sir Jack Da Vinci and B.C. Ethic.

North Beach   **415-392-1522**
1412 Grant Avenue   Mon-Tues 11-7, Wed 11-8
San Francisco 94133   Thurs-Sat 11-10, Sun 12-6

On the Run

Aptly named, this straightforward and spacious neighborhood shoe store supports the minds and soles of urban trekkers and athletes with its feel-good collection of walking, hiking and running shoes and equally supportive customer service. A huge selection of ecco, Dansko, BeautiFeel, Durea, 1803, Josef Seibeo, Mephisto, Stonefly and customized insoles has secured the spacious stomping ground's cult status among sure-footed shoppers.

Sunset **415-665-5311**
1310 9th Avenue Mon-Sat 10-6:30
San Francisco 94122 Sun 11-5

☆ Ooma

Step into an explosion of color when you enter this playful, pop fashion stop—definitely not the place for those who think style means black. Former dot-commer Kate Logan created Ooma (Object Of My Affection) to showcase over 25 local designers (Miss Fitt & Co, Paola, Kiki Stash) as well as better known designers like Trina Turk, Milly and Edward An. Tucked among all the fun fashion finds are also great accessories, jewelry and gifts. And if that wasn't enough, the store offers validated parking at a nearby lot—a real bonus in this auto-overloaded neighborhood. www.ooma.net

North Beach **415-627-6963**
1422 Grant Avenue Tues-Sat 11-7
San Francisco 94133 Sun 12-6

Ovation

You may not look twice at this somewhat bland-looking boutique, but fashion-minded Marina maidens do. They then fill up from the stock of Belly tees, Michael Stars tees, French Connection dresses, trendy Trina Turk urban basics and decent party duds. www.ovationclothing.com

Marina **415-931-5445**
2124 Chestnut Street Mon-Fri 11-7, Sat-Sun 10-6
San Francisco 94123

Berkeley **510-652-9111**
3206 College Avenue Mon-Thus 10-6, Fri 11-7
Berkeley 94705 Sat 10-6, Sun 12-5

Paolo

Turn right off the Fillmore shopping strip and find this whimsical shop full of Paolo Iantorno's funky chic shoes. The columns, texture-splashed walls with faux window shutters and Roman stone statues evoke a Florentine street feel, a perfectly fun backdrop for his fashion-forward soles (Miu Miu-like, but with his own flavor and without those sky-high prices). Also find shapes from Roberto Rinaldi and handbags from Arcadia. Their second shop snuck into fashion-forward Hayes Valley just under a year ago. www.paoloshoes.com

Pacific Heights **415-885-5701**
1971 Sutter Street Daily 11-7 (Sun 12-6)
San Francisco 94115

Directory

Hayes Valley   **415-552-4580**
524 Hayes Street   (opening times as above)
San Francisco 94102

Patagonia

Adventure hounds who paddle, peddle, surf, ski and scale big rocks can't get enough at this outdoorsy outlet. Patagoniacs love to stockpile the flexible and form-fitting tops, polypropylene underlayers, wind-resistant jackets and irresistible fleece before meeting up with Mother Nature. A great stop for world travelers, world-class athletes, backcountry explorers, bikers and surfers, or really anyone who favors life out of bounds (or wants to look like they do).   www.patagonia.com

Fisherman's Wharf   **415-771-2050**
770 North Point Sun 11-5, Mon-Tues, Fri-Sat 10-6
San Francisco 94109   Wed-Thurs 10-7

Paul Frank

When Julius and friends landed on Haight Street in 2000, Paul Frank fans went berserk. It was the kooky cartoonist's first foray into retail—he has since opened stores across the US and in London and Japan. His flagship SF store now has these fancy downtown digs—four times larger than the original and his biggest store in the world. Judging from the throngs clamoring for his pleather backpacks, cat-splashed T-shirts and signature monkey-front garb, the store, complete with a space-age TV rolling his animation, is a huge success.   www.paulfrank.com

Union Square   **415-374-2758**
262 Sutter Street Daily 10-7 (Sun 11-6)
San Francisco 94111

Peluche

The well turned-out career woman gets her fix at these small specialty shops. Look for the classics, tailored suits with skirts and pants, blouses and accessories to boot. Sexy diva dresses sure to seduce the Southern California set also lure seductresses to this place.

Cow Hollow   **415-441-2505**
1954 Union Street Daily 11-6 (Sun 11-5)
San Francisco 94123

Peninsula   **650-579-4606**
348 Lorton Avenue Daily 10:30-6 (Sun 10-3)
Burlingame 94010

Piedmont

This mecca for all things fabulously flamboyant has been the first stop for strippers, transvestites, costume partygoers and Burning Man revelers since 1972. In this ultimate ode to the ornamental you'll find all that glitters—from pasties, rhinestone bras, panties, a rainbow of cowboy hats, garter belts, and men's and women's g-strings to fetish favorites, leopardskin Lycra pants, garish gowns, feather boas and classic hosiery. Every possible accessory is also here, from eyelashes and wigs to costume jewelry and belts. Great prices, too. www.piedmontsf.com

Haight-Ashbury 415-864-8075
1452 Haight Street Daily 11-7
San Francisco 94117

Positively Haight Street

Sightseers searching for their inner Haight-Ashbury hippy rush this corner tie-dye emporium loaded with kaleido-scope T-shirts, crochet bags, crepe pants, posters, silver rings, scarves and groovy ethnic clothes.

Haight-Ashbury 415-252-8747
1400 Haight Street Daily 10-8 (Sun 11-7)
San Francisco 94117

Prada

The much-talked about Rem Koolhaas-designed Prada project on Post Street was due to open in 2003 but has been on hold with no news of a completion date. In the meantime, this former Ultimo space has been tinted with the fashionista-familiar mint-green hue to temporarily nour-ish Pradanistas with its continuous wave of with-it wear, heels and bags. www.prada.com

Union Square 415-391-8844
140 Geary Street Mon-Sat 10-6
San Francisco 94108

Puma

The glowing panther leaping off a fiery red wall signals your arrival at perpetually hip Puma, which after its resurgence again inspires the sporty set to pounce on the latest pave-ment pounders. The souped-up space from the German sneaker-maker stocks all the colorful cutting-edge treads and athleticwear that have helped kick-start sportif style into its à la mode era. www.puma.com

Union Square 415-788-9880
856 Market Street Daily 10-9 (Sun 10-7)
San Francisco 94103

Rabat

A reliable shoe source for trendy types who don't necessar-ily want to put all their savings into their soles, just some. Rabat's two locales are brimming with boots, mules and pumps from old reliables like Robert Clergerie, Stephane Kélian, Giraudon, Espace and a slew of other lesser-known but equally chic names. The Marina and Noe Valley shops also carry contemporary womenswear like Nanette Lepore, Cop Copine, Save the Queen, and Betsey Johnson.

Noe Valley 415-282-7861
4001 24th Street Mon-Fri 10-6:30
San Francisco 94114 Sat 10-6, Sun 11-5:30

Marina	**415-929-8868**
2080 Chestnut Street	Mon-Fri 10:30-6:30
San Francisco 94123	Sat 10:30-6, Sun 11-5:30
Berkeley	**510-549-9195**
1825 4th Street	Mon-Fri 10-6, Sat 10-6, Sun 11-5:30
Berkeley 94710	

The Rafaels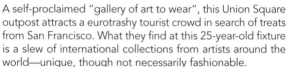

A self-proclaimed "gallery of art to wear", this Union Square outpost attracts a eurotrashy tourist crowd in search of treats from San Francisco. What they find at this 25-year-old fixture is a slew of international collections from artists around the world—unique, though not necessarily fashionable.

Union Square	**415-974-6772**
643 Market Street	Mon-Sat 10-6
San Francisco 94105	
Union Square	**415-956-3489**
285 Geary Street	Mon-Sat 10-6
San Francisco 94102	

Ralph Lauren

The well-heeled and Waspy have been filling their wardrobes with Ralph's tweeds, polos, blazers and Oscar-quality formalwear for 35 years. The haute American lifestyle brand, all yachtsy, rugged, outdoorsy and lock-jawed features an entire world of sharp, smart and sophisticated ready-to-wear, sportswear, accessories and vintage jewelry—the personification of preppy chic.   www.polo.com

Union Square	**415-788-7656**
Crocker Galleria	Mon-Sat 10-6
90 Post Street	San Francisco 94104
Peninsula	**650-326-1710**
Stanford Shopping Center	Mon-Fri 10-9, Sat 10-7
Palo Alto 94304	Sun 11-6

Redfive

With Haight Street's move from hippy to hip-hop, this current kid on the block is right in step with the neighborhood's fresh vibe. High-end streetwear is what owners Erik Ross and Josh Fishel are retailing. That means T-shirts with "deeper meanings", political messages and Seventies icons from underground designers like Addict, Sarcastic and Redfive's own line, which also includes a full set of streetwise sportswear. Music magazines like *Tokion* are for sale, and be sure to check back every six weeks for new artwork on exhibit.   www.redfiveonline.com

Haight-Ashbury	**415-552-6494**
1472 Haight Street	Daily 11-7
San Francisco 94117	

REI

Outdoor enthusiasts with down-to-earth energy count on REI (short for Recreational Equipment Incorporated) for all their camping, climbing, kayaking, fishing and general out-side adventure equipment. The cooperative-run company (become a member and receive year-end refunds) carries all the top-of-the-line gear, plus their own-label clothing and accoutrements.   www.rei.com

Berkeley   **510-527-4140**
1338 San Pablo Avenue   Mon-Fri 10-9, Sat 10-8, Sun 10-7
Berkeley 94702

Marin   **415-927-1938**
213 Corte Madera Town Center   Mon-Fri 10-9, Sat 10-7
Corte Madera 94925   Sun 11-6

Retro Fit Vintage

Retro mammas and papas dig this stylishly groovy haunt. The vintage vibe is eclectic, chic and decidedly hip, a place where browning *Playboys* mix with Technicolor wigs, old rock shirts, rows of fab Sixties coats and clothes that groovy grandma used to wear. Owners Alison Hoekstra and Audrey Wackerly handpick the goods that span the Forties to the Seventies and even the ostentatious Eighties.   www.retrofitclothing.com

Mission   **415-550-1530**
910 Valencia Street   Mon, Wed, Sun 12-6
San Francisco 94110   Thurs 1:30-7, Fri 12-7, Sat 12-8

Reva Mivasagar: The Guild

This Australian (New York-based) designer's San Francisco store delights dare-to-be-different brides with her unique ivory creations. Mivasagar sculpts duchesse satin into opera coats and whips silk and organza into beautiful, bil-lowing gowns in a number of styles. Don't be dismayed by the dingy-looking samples, many a chic bride has been in and out of them. Also find a small selection of elegant eveningwear.

Union Square   **415-981-3301**
375 Grant Avenue, 3rd Floor   Tues-Fri 12-6, Sat 10-6
San Francisco 94108

Ria Shoes

To the relief of those tourists stomping around Union Square all day long, Ria shoes come to the rescue. Packed with comfortable walkers for guys and gals, the store has a sizeable selection of footwear from Caterpillar, Clarks, Mephisto, Sebago, Arche, Teva and Merrell. Be it clogs, chunky thumpers, hiking boots or just cushy walkers, these shops are sure to stock it. Look for sale items upstairs.

Union Square   **415-834-1420**
301 Grant Avenue   Daily 9:30-6:30 (Sun 10-6)
San Francisco 94108

Union Square   **415-398-0895**
437 Sutter Street   Daily 9:30-6
San Francisco 94108

Riki

From Davis-based designer Ursula Labermeier comes this cool Northern California line steeped with European flavor (from Labermeier's German roots). Once a North Beach haunt, this boutique now on both sides of the Bay houses her moderately priced and timelessly hip separates—bias-cut skirts, bootleg pants, casual capris—infused with the season's trends without being too trendy. Ella, her wholesale collection (a more generously cut Riki), also hangs here, along with Frederic handbags and Franco Sarto shoes. www.rikifashion.com

Noe Valley   **415-641-4407**
4037 24th Street   Daily 11-6:30 (Sun 12-6)
San Francisco 94114

Berkeley   **510-540-5557**
2111 Vine Street   Mon-Fri 10-6, Sat-Sun 12-6
Berkeley 94704

☆ Riley James

Named after the owner's high-strung hound (a Chihuahua who nervously escorts shoppers around the store), this upstairs boutique has everything a sophisticated and flirty girl needs to go from day into evening—Fifties-inspired dresses from Jill Michelle, in-demand Alvin Valley pants and casual suits by Rebecca Taylor and Chaiken. Hollywould shoes and leather goods by local designer Nelly Mack round out the selection. And there's even a small section of menswear for your favorite beau.

Cow Hollow   **415 775 7956**
3027 Fillmore Street   Mon-Sat 11-8, Sun 12-6
San Francisco 94123

Rin

Trendy neighborhood gals are happy to take a few steps down (below street level, that is) to find their favorite feminine fashions from independent lines like Development, Blue Colt Jeans, Ya Ya, In the Now and James Perse. Owner Rin Chon also keeps her customers coming back with hot hats by Eugenia Kim, jewelry by local designers and comfy low-rise undies by Underglam.

Cow Hollow   **415-922-8040**
2111 Union Street   Mon-Sat 11-7
San Francisco 94123   Sun 12-6

Rockport

Forget fancy footwear. This performance-shoe purveyor is all about form and function and has been selling its sturdy soles, made specifically for strolling, since 1971. Engineers of walking comfort in even dressier designs, Rockport also turns out golf shoes, sneakers, belts, bags and rugged casual clothes. Rockport believes that comfort starts at your feet, a philosophy fashionistas find tough to follow. www.rockport.com

Union Square   **415-951-4801**
165 Post Street   Daily 10-7 (Sun 12-6)
San Francisco 94108

Rolo 450

With five stores scattered around the city, all carrying completely different stock, Rolo covers just about every category of hip. This one has a fiercely stylish Castro set stomping in for the freshest streetwear looks. Find lines like Energie, Nice Collective, Ben Sherman and Levi's and a rad choice of shoes from Tsubo, Pro-Keds and Vans.   www.rolo.com

Castro   **415-626-7171**
450 Castro Street   Daily 11-8 (Sun 11-7)
San Francisco 94114

Rolo on Market

Fashion-forward guys are devoted to this temple of designer duds. The most upscale of the Rolo roster, this store features up-to-the-nanosecond styles from a quality crew that's edgy (Helmut Lang, Comme des Garçons, G-Star) and upscale urban (Dolce & Gabbana, Paul Smith). And what trendster can survive without cool cosmetics? A must-have Kiehl's collection is also housed here.   www.rolo.com

Castro   **415-431-4545**
2351 Market Street   Daily 11-8 (Sun 11-7)
San Francisco 94114

Directory

Rolo Garage

Those familiar with all five Rolo outposts love to scour their most secret spot—this South of Market outlet—for hipper-than-hip goodies at discounted prices (20-50% off). Find shreds of leftovers from each of the boutiques: high-end designers, streetwear, underwear, outerwear and shoes.   www.rolo.com

SoMa   **415-861-2097**
1301 Howard Street   Daily 11-7
San Francisco 94103

Rolo Undercover

What started as an underwear and swimwear store is now a treasure house of fashion-forward togs that include club-going gear and jeans too. Bits of womenswear are scattered about the guy goods which cater to this hip 'hood, heavy on boys. Among the So Low undies, find plenty of sheer, tight, vinyl and python pieces.   www.rolo.com

Castro   **415-864-0505**
545 Castro Street   Mon-Thurs 11:30-7:30
San Francisco 94114   Fri-Sat 11-8, Sun 11:30-7

☆ Rolo SoMa

This loft-like space offers hip urban shoppers the opportunity to have a cup of coffee while they shop for specialty denim. For guys, find names like G-Star, Paper Denim & Cloth, Nice Collective and Rogan; for gals, much of the same plus Miss Sixty, A G Jeans and Joe's Jeans.   www.rolo.com

SoMa   **415-355-1122**
1235 Howard Street   Daily 11-7
San Francisco 94103

Romantasy Exquisite Corsetry   🛉

The top spot for custom corsetry from eight exquisite designers, this out-of-the-way web- and catalog-based biz with personal fittings available by appointment makes waist cinching downright sexy. Laced-up lusciousness comes in every form from playful plastic waist-pinchers and elaborate Scarlett O'Hara size-slimmers to Victorian visions, lascivious leather numbers and contemporary bust boosters. Order online or call for custom fitting, but either way it'll cost you. Prices start at around $400.   www.romantasy.com

Glen Park	**415-585-0760**
2912 Diamond Street, suite 239	(by appointment only)
San Francisco 94131	

Ross Dress for Less   🛉🛉🛉

Tired of doling out for department-store prices? SF-based Ross, no less daunting in size, hawks big-brand designer duds at 20-60% off regular rates. The best deals seem to spring out of the sportswear department (you might spot great goods from Jones New York, Tommy Hilfiger, Liz Claiborne or Polo Ralph Lauren); sifting through the dresses can prove much more taxing.   www.rossstores.com

Union Square	**415-957-9222**
799 Market Street	Mon-Fri 9:30-9
San Francisco 94103	Sat 9:30-8, Sun 11-6
Richmond	**415-386-7677**
5200 Geary Boulevard	Daily 9:30-9 (Sun 10-6)
San Francisco 94121	
Nob Hill	**415-775-0192**
1645 Van Ness Avenue	Daily 9:30-9 (Sun 11-7)
San Francisco 94109	
Berkeley	**510-549-9761**
2190 Shattuck Avenue	Daily 9:30-8 (Sun 11-6)
Berkeley 94704	
Marin	**415-332-0519**
194 Donahue Street	Daily 9:30-9:30 (Sun 11-7)
Marin City 94965	

Ruby Gallery   🛉

Starting with only six designers six years ago, Laura James now showcases a whopping 50 in her homey little shop— or "accessories gallery" as she calls it. A supporter of local artists, James counts fake-fur hats from wiG, bead-handled handbags from DAS and silver and sea-glass rings from Catherine Weitzman among her SF designer roster. Old tunes croon in the crafty shop, which is a sure bet for chic and unique finds.   www.rubygallery.com

Mission	**415-550-8052**
3602 20th Street	Mon 3-8, Tues 3-9, Wed-Fri 12-7
San Francisco 94110	Sat-Sun 11-6

The Sak   🛉

This stark white stop with huge glass windows in the Union Square area houses all Elliott Lucca's lovely sacs. Check the cubbyhole displays for his latest shoulder bags and purses, from straw numbers to wooded mesh to crochet carriers and his signature Tightweave totes. Also find belts and woven cosmetic and glass cases.   www.thesak.com

Union Square   **415-433-3100**
334 Grant Avenue   Daily 10-7 (Sun 11-6)
San Francisco 94108

Saks Fifth Avenue

This is one of the classiest places to graze on the latest fashion looks. The chic set ignores the anti-glam interior and heads straight for the refined selections from the European and American runways. They also feed on a stellar assortment of bridge lines, cosmetics, wonderful accessories and footwear. Don't miss the expanded downstairs shoe department, which doubled its size in the past year, and the big boy's store down the street.   www.saksfifthavenue.com

Union Square   **415-986-4300**
384 Post Street   Mon-Sat 10-7 (Thurs 10-8)
San Francisco 94108   Sun 11-6

Saks Men's Store

Ground zero for à la mode menswear, this handsome wood-paneled place with art deco details keeps the stylish set swathed in Versace, Gaultier, Armani, Prada and a cornucopia of other legendary names. Outstanding, humble service makes this most modern Saks one of the classiest men's outfits in the city. Hike to the fifth floor for the cutting-edge assortment.

Union Square   **415-986-4300**
220 Post Street   Mon-Sat 10-7 (Thurs 10-8)
San Francisco 94108   Sun 11-6

Salvatore Ferragamo

Sophisticated Italian style is what this Florentine family delivers season upon season. Thanks to Marc Audibet, who headed up design in recent years, the somewhat conservative collection of ready-to-wear took on a refreshingly smarter air. Since his spring 2002 departure Graeme Black, formerly of Ralph Lauren, stepped into his styling shoes. Shoe maestri since the days when Salvatore custom-cut Audrey Hepburn's heels, Ferragamo is still a name synonymous with contemporary, elegant and reliable soles, bags and small leather goods.   www.ferragamo.com

Union Square   **415-391-6565**
233 Geary Street   Mon-Fri 10:30-7
San Francisco 94102   Sun 12-6

Sarah Shaw

Another option for maidens à la mode. Shaw (not to be confused with the LA handbag designer) also owns the shoe gallery Fetish up the street and caters to all the best-dressed girls in this yuppity neighborhood. A young SF stylite herself, this retail queen carries the usual urban-chic suspects—Tom K. Nguyen, Trina Turk, Juicy Couture, Autumn Cashmere—and plenty of party frocks for Pacific Heights players.

Pacific Heights　　　　　　　　**415-929-2990**
3095 Sacramento Street　　　　Daily 10-6 (Sun 11-5)
San Francisco 94115

Satellite Vintage

This vintage shop on a clothing-barren block of Haight Street offers a limited but delicious assortment of Thirties-to-early-Eighties garb. If you're in the market for a suede patchwork coat, embroidered silk Mandarin jacket, Thirties fox-trimmed number, leather blazer or Sixties car coat, check in with owners Jason and Jacki to see what they've got up their swanky sleeves.　　www.satellitevintage.com

Haight-Ashbury　　　　　　　　**415-626-1364**
1364 Haight Street　　　　　Mon-Fri 12-7, Sat 11-7
San Francisco 94117　　　　　　　　Sun 12-6:30

Schauplatz

Groovy guys and dolls delve into this retro world cooked up by Bernhard Wetsch and Alan Freedman. This is the place for boas and leopard bags, cat-eye glasses and handpicked threads from the Forties, Fifties, Sixties and Seventies. A standout in the vintage universe, Schauplatz (German for happening place) also peddles pumps and used publishing material.

Mission　　　　　　　　　　**415-864-5665**
791 Valencia Street　　　　　　　　Tues-Sun 12-7
San Francisco 94110

Scheuer Linens

Three generations of Scheuers have ensured San Franciscans sleep soundly on lovely bed linens in pretty patterns and pamper their pads with tasteful towels, scented laundry detergents and other haute accoutrements for the home. Loungers love the wooden wardrobe at the back of the store that's packed with more mature classic nighties (including a large selection of Veréna), exotic silk robes and hard-to-find quilted bed-jackets.

Union Square　　　　　　　　**415-392-2813**
340 Sutter Street　　　　　　Mon-Sat 9:30-5:30
San Francisco 94108

Sean

Fans of the creative-casual look seek out this shoebox of a store, which loyally stocks the rich-tinted tops, pants and painters' jackets of French designer Pierre Emile Lafaurie. There are also plenty of suits and a variety of sportswear to feed any neighborhood yuppy's fashionable wardrobe.

Cow Hollow　　　　　　　　**415-474-7363**
1749 Union Street　　　　　Mon-Fri 11-7, Sat 10-7
San Francisco 94123　　　　　　　　Sun 12-6

See Jane Run

This place peddles labels you can get almost anywhere, really, but SJR has an athletic girl-power vibe that can't be beat. Finely edited with the best apparel, shoes and accessories for female fitness freaks, the neighborhood shop is a girly gearhead's dream. Find Patagonia, Moving Comfort, Prana and Hind for cyclists, swimmers, hikers, runners and yoginis. www.seejanerunsports.com

Noe Valley	**415-401-8338**
3870 24th Street	Mon-Fri 11-7, Sat 10-6
San Francisco 94114	Sun 11-5

Oakland	**510-428-2681**
5817 College Avenue	Mon-Fri 11-7, Sat 10-6
Oakland 94618	Sun 12-5

Selix

It's hardly haute stuff, but downtown dudes know this rather glum gray space is a sure thing for straightforward men's formalwear at straight-up prices. Rentals and sales include selections from Bill Blass, Perry Ellis, Chaps Ralph Lauren, Oscar de la Renta, After Six and Raffinati as well as accoutrements (shoes, ties, cuff links) to turn today's schoolboy into tonight's prom prince. www.selix.com

Union Square	**415-362-1133**
123 Kearny Street	Mon-Fri 10-7, Sat 8:30-5
San Francisco 94108	

Sunset	**415-333-2412**
2622 Ocean Avenue	Mon-Fri 10-7, Sat 9-5
San Francisco 94132	Sun 12-4

Marin	**415-455-0830**
874 4th Street	Mon-Fri 10-7, Sat 8:30-5
San Rafael 94901	

Oakland	**510-452-2751**
1724 Broadway	Mon-Fri 9-7, Sat 8:30-5
Oakland 94612	

Shaw Shoes

Don't mind the shoddy, aged interior of this Union Street fixture. Shaw has been selling shoes to a chichi crew for over three decades and still carries plenty of cool heels. The seductive stock of sandals, shoes and boots ranges from inexpensive (Me Too) to haute (Clergerie, Casadei and Charles Jourdan).

Cow Hollow	**415-922-5676**
2001 Union Street	Daily 11-7 (Sun 12:30-5:30)
San Francisco 94123	

She

Pronounced "she-he" and representative of the male/female fashions stocked at this funky store, She is the brainchild of Jeffrey Allen and Joseph Pinizzotto who serve up a small selection of not-too-pricey pieces for each of the sexes. Modly madeover recently in soft champagne pink, this place carries dress-up, dress-down duds from Poleci and Anna Huling for her, Parke & Ronen and Ike & Dean for him.

Hayes Valley   **415-552-4030**
528 Hayes Street   Mon 12-6, Tues-Sat 11-7
San Francisco 94102   Sun 11-6

ShoeBiz

Cornering all the feet stomping around Haight Street, this trio of shoe stores caters to every kind of crowd. There's an athletic-inspired shop selling Hyde, Gravis and Puma sneaks, an urban-trendy outpost with Nine West and other sexy, sandaly knock-offs and a chicer and more expensive emporium hawking Cydwoq, BCBG max azria and Camper's fashionable footwear.   www.shoebizsf.com

Haight-Ashbury   **415-861-0313**
1422 Haight Street   Daily 11-7 (Sun 11-6)
San Francisco 94117

Haight-Ashbury   **415-864-0990**
1446 Haight Street   Mon-Sat 11-7, Sun 12-6
San Francisco 94117

Haight-Ashbury   **415-861-3933**
1553 Haight Street   (opening times as above)
San Francisco 94117

Shoesizes

The self-described "hard to find size and width specialist" swung open its Marina corner doors last spring, luring all tourists, athletes, walkers and neighborhood folks with funky-sized feet. Find oversize, wide and extra-wide pairs of sneakers, boots and other comfortable soles from brands like New Balance, Timberland, Rockport, Kenneth Cole, Clarks and Birkenstock. Feet of more usual measurements can also find decent footwear here.   www.shoesizes.com

Marina   **415-474-1931**
2798 Lombard Street   Mon-Fri 10:30-6:30
San Francisco 94123   Sat 10:30-6 (Sun 12-5)

Skechers USA

San Franciscans have been sporting these street-savvy stompers since the California company's inception in 1992. Now that Rob Lowe, Britney Spears and Matt Dillon have promoted the line, teenyboppers to *West Wing* addicts are walking in their signature wavy designs of colorful sneakers, leather boots, and platform sandals and shoes. Look for the Skechers Collection, a line of men's dress and casual footwear too.   www.skechers.com

Union Square   **415-781-8703**
770 Market Street   Mon-Sat 10-8
San Francisco 94102   Sun 11-6

Mission   **415-401-6211**
2600 Mission Street   Daily 10-7 (Sun 11-6)
San Francisco 94110

Sisley

This revolutionary brand started in Paris in 1968 but by the Seventies was part of the Benetton family. It's still the hipper, edgier collection of guys' and gals' gear. From microminis to leather jackets, everything is exclusively made in Italy. www.sisley.com

Union Square 415-392-8900
59 Grant Avenue Daily 11-7 (Sun 12-6)
San Francisco 94108

Directory

Small Frys

Owner Carol Yenne, a former Levi Strauss marketing manager, took over this neighborhood kids' fashion haven in 1990. The cloud-painted place is, naturally, loaded with mini Levi's—jeans and jackets—in addition to OshKosh overalls, a rainbow of T-shirts, shorts, dresses, sleepwear and other affordable play clothes, many from West Coast companies. Also find other whimsical baby accoutrements, from dishes to stuffed animals. www.smallfrys.com

Noe Valley 415-648-3954
4066 24th Street Mon-Sat 10-6 (Fri 10-7)
San Francisco 94114 Sun 11-5:30

Smash Footwear

One of the sleekest Marina stores, this shoe shop lures a pretty, pedicured and posh posse in search of swanky soles. All thanks to the stock of Sigerson Morrison, Stephane Kélian, Puma, Gun Metal and Freelance, neatly tucked into stark white cubby cases. You will also find the occasional handbag collection and wallets from Stephane Kélian.

Marina 415-673-4736
2030 Chestnut Street Daily 11-6:30 (Sun 12-5)
San Francisco 94123

☆ Smith Williams

The only things more handsome than North Carolina brothers Claiborne and Smith Williams who opened this streamlined menagerie of fitted fashion-forward menswear in 2001 are the edgy European-style clothes they sell. The distinctive fashions, which are designed by Smith and made in Italy, are meant for the twentyfive-to-fortysomething man who's not afraid to dress with flair. Check out their case for Ian Flaherty cufflinks and wall of inlaid boxes with handmade Botti shoes. www.smithwilliamsstores.com

Cow Hollow 415-346-4280
1827 Union Street Daily 10-7 (Sun 11-6)
San Francisco 94123

Sparky's Vintage Clothing

Fedora-donning hep cats and Deluxe bar regulars know this is the place to load up on yesterday's fashions for tomorrow's smooth look. Owner Das Anastasiou keeps the racks well hung with classics from the Fifties to the Seventies, especially in regard to Hawaiian shirts and new and vintage western wear, plus Forties men's ties. A few shelves are dedicated to Fifties Lucite purses, Bakelite jewelry, and space toys.

Haight-Ashbury　　　　　　　　　　　**415-387-5053**
1764 Haight Street　　　　　　　　　　　Daily 11-7
San Francisco 94117

St. John

Nob Hill's grand dames are giddy since this 40-year-old American-traditional fashion house opened its location in the Four Seasons Hotel in 2002. Designer Marie Gray's contemporary suits, elegant eveningwear, shoes and bags are more modern genteel, while sportswear, jewelry and home accessories are classically conservative.

Union Square　　　　　　　　　　　**415-856-0420**
767 Market Street　　　　　Mon-Sat 10-6 (Thurs 10-7)
San Francisco 94103　　　　　　　　　　Sun 12-5

Steve Madden

Chunky and clunky describe the kind of shoes Steve Madden delivers. Young punks count on sky-high thumpers, mostly of the platform phylum—sandals, sneakers, Mary Janes, boots and pumps with cork or wooden soles. Wacky and wild, these risers are tamer in the price-tag department.　　　　　　　　www.stevemadden.com

Union Square　　　　　　　　　　　**415-777-2430**
San Francisco Shopping Centre　Mon-Sat 9:30-8, Sun 11-6
865 Market Street　　　　　　　　San Francisco 94103

Stormy Leather

The tough and kinky get their kicks in this wild world of leather. Most of the merchandise comes from the cheeky boutique's own label, but also find a smattering of other names. Vests, jackets, jeans, harnesses and a full-on leather bordello with corsets, spikes and such keep a butchy bunch well clad.　　　　　　　　　www.stormyleather.com

SoMa　　　　　　　　　　　　　**415-626-1672**
1158 Howard Street　　　　　　　　　　Daily 12-7
San Francisco 94103

Studio On Chestnut

Blue-chip conservatives like to stock up on the basic pants, shirts and simple no-nonsense style at this Chestnut Street shop. If you can't be bothered by fussy fashion or are rather unresponsive to runway trends, this Eileen Fisher-filled store is a great bet for you.

Marina　　　　　　　　　　　　**415-776-5078**
2233 Chestnut Street　　　　Mon-Fri 10:30-6, Sat 10-5
San Francisco 94123

Stüssy

Like the street-smart kids who were once seduced by Stüssy's graphics and hip-hop vibe, this urban byword has matured. A sleek new sense of street, skate, design and technology has swept through the line and through the stores, like this one which opened in 2002. Find all the caps, messenger bags, T-shirts and pants that blend skate with workwear, preppy attitude and surplus, still splashed with the discernible screen-printed signature.   www.stussy.com

Haight-Ashbury   **415-701-7474**
1409 Haight Street   Daily 11-7 (Sun 11-6)
San Francisco 94117

☆ Subterranean Shoe Room

This shoebox of a shop with a mammoth subterranean future is the place to track down vintage trainers. Be it old Air Jordans, never-worn, hard-to-find Pumas or ancient Adidas, the brothers Bingaman probably stock it in this stripped-down Mission haunt. These sneaker freaks also sell new and old Frye boots, bowling-inspired and other unusual treads, and custom-made boots.   www.subshoeroom.com

Mission   **415-401-9504**
877 Valencia Street   Daily 12-7
San Francisco 94110

☆ Sugar Poppy

Nob Hill gals were thrilled when this fun fem shop hung out its bright pink awning in 2001. One of the few fashion stops in the neighborhood, it's sating shoppers with an eclectic mix of clothes, accessories and gifts all in a fun retro girl-party environment. Owner Catherine Montalbo says she caters to "the woman who doesn't follow the crowd" but that doesn't mean she doesn't also carry hot labels like Blue Cult, Ashe Francombe, Urchin and Custo. Look for a small collection of vintage items mixed in for good measure.   www.sugarpoppy.com

Nob Hill   **415-775-4979**
1552 Polk Street   Mon-Fri 11-8
San Francisco 94109   Sat 11-7, Sun 12-6

Sugar Pussy

Whether you're a stripper or just like to dress like one, this shop is the first stop on the hoochie-mama express. This sexy boutique carries an equal mix of lingerie and tantaliz-ing streetwear from companies like Custo Barcelona, GSUS, Sergio Valente and Fine, plus owner Jennifer Summer's sig-nature Sugarpussy line.   www.sugarpussclothing.com

Haight-Ashbury   **415-861-PUSS**
248 Fillmore Street   Mon-Sat 12-7
San Francisco 94117   Sun 12-6 (Summer only)

Sugar Shack

San Francisco may often be blanketed with fog, but it's always Palm Beach in summertime within Katherine Ryan and Robin Weisburg's ultra-bright boutique featuring the West Coast's largest collection of Lilly Pulitzer-designed resortwear. A swirl of vibrant smocks accompanies tropical-print tees, sorbet-colored shorts, sunshine-summoning slacks and children's wear perfect for the Marin poolside party.   www.shopatsugarshack.com

Cow Hollow
1858 Union Street
San Francisco 94123

415-775-0119
Daily 10-7 (Sun 11-6)

Sunhee Moon

This SF indie designer lures a cool young coterie to her minimalist pad in the Lower Haight. The spare space with black-stained hardwood floors and crisp white walls houses Moon's classically hip line of polo tops, cropped pants, basic blouses, sleek trenches and boot-cut pants, all at digestible prices. Also find a smattering of sunglasses, candles and local handmade jewelry. www.sunheemoon.com.

Haight-Ashbury
142 Fillmore Street
San Francisco 94117

415-355-1800
Daily 12-6 (Sat-Sun 12-5)

☆ Susan

Status-conscious style hounds frequent this Presidio Heights boutique for one thing only, designer duds. Apart from picks from the cream of the fashion crop—Alexander McQueen, Prada, Marni, John Galliano—this posh place is known for its preying and sometimes pretentious sales staff. But don't be put off, this really is the best place to pick up the international labels. Yohji and Comme des Garçons devotees won't be disappointed...their dark, stark, most outrageous numbers seem to be owner Susan Foslien's weakness.

Presidio Heights
3685 Sacramento Street
San Francisco 94118

415-922-3685
Mon-Sat 10:30-6:30

Peninsula
1403 Burlingame Avenue
Burlingame 94010

650-347-0452
Mon-Sat 10-6

Talbots

The preppy set always seems to have a taste for Talbots. The East Coast institution continues to deliver comfy career clothes through its massive mail-order biz and these buttoned-up boutiques, as it has for over 50 years. Middle-aged professionals and young prepsters pine for their Irish linen jackets, plaid pants, gingham outfits, spiffy formalwear and casual sportswear in a wide range of sizes (4-24), including a sizeable petites department. www.talbots.com

Union Square
128 Post Street
San Francisco 94108

415-398-8881
Mon-Wed, Fri-Sat 10-6
Thurs 10-7, Sun 12-5

Sunset
Stonestown Galleria
3251 20th Avenue

415-566-7311
Daily 10-9 (Sun 11-6)
San Francisco 94132

Marin
Village at Corte Madera
1500 Redwood Highway
Corte Madera 94925

415-927-3793
Mon-Fri 10-9, Sat 10-7:30
Sun 11-6

Marin (petites)   **415-924-1799**
Village at Corte Madera   (opening times as above)
1502 Redwood Highway   Corte Madera 94925

Peninsula   **650-289-9151**
Stanford Shopping Center   Mon-Fri 10-9, Sat 10-7
Palo Alto 94304   Sun 11-6

Therapy

Geared toward the neighborhood's fashionably funky set, this is the one-stop shop for edgy, affordable streetwear. Behind an eclectic collection of cards, kooky gifts, and retro robots the racks reveal staples like Dickies, Free People, Nisa, Private Circle and Paul Frank. Men migrate toward the Ben Sherman separates and utility bags. Fashion hounds know this is handbag heaven, including the durable but chic Detroit bag woven from seatbelts. The sister location focuses on furnishings.

Mission   **415-861-6213**
545 Valencia Street   Mon-Thurs 12-9
San Francisco 94110   Fri-Sat 12-11, Sun 11-7

Mission   **415-621-5902**
758 Valencia Street   Daily 12-7
San Francisco 94110

Third Hand Store

John Galliano and Catherine Deneuve are only two of the fashion legends who have foraged Divisadero's nondescript strip for vintage with va-va-vroom. Owner Joseph Dowler's high-quality hand-me-downs from the Twenties through the Forties add extra kick to today's flappers and debonair gents. Also check out the great bygone bridal selection.

Western Addition   **415-567-7332**
1839 Divisadero Street   Mon-Sat 12-6
San Francisco 94115

This Little Piggy Wears Cotton

Frolic through this store with your wee bunch (infants to age 12) and pick from the top-notch kiddie clothes (think One Kid, Petit Bateau, Charlie Rocket, Flapdoodles, Baby Lulu), jewelry and antique furnishings. The Santa Barbara-based company also commissions crop tops, two-piece sets and smocked dresses aptly embellished with little piggies or other farm animals.   www.littlepiggy.com

Berkeley   **510-981-1411**
1840 4th Street   Daily 10-6 (Sun 11-6)
Berkeley 94710

Thomas Pink

In a strategic spot near SF's financial district, this classic British outpost is a must for men on a shirt mission. The fitted shirts, button-downs, oxfords and spread collars in rich Egyptian cotton and poplin all have their appointed slots, color-coded in a meticulous spread. TP also spins a women's collection of tailored tops in feel-good fabrics like linen and cotton.   www.thomaspink.com

Union Square 415-421-2022
255 Post Street Mon-Fri 10-7, Sat 10-6
San Francisco 94108 Sun 11-6

Three Bags Full ♂♀

With an inventory of more than 400 handmade sweaters, these small specialty stores are a knit nut's paradise. With 24 years of experience, the SF-based retailers boast a bundle of cardigans and pullovers from English and American knitters, many designed exclusively for the shops. From cashmere and cotton to rayon chenille and microfibers, they come in all shapes, sizes, patterns, jacquards and simple solids. www.threebagsfull.com

Cow Hollow 415-567-5753
2181 Union Street Daily10:30-5 (Sun 12-5)
San Francisco 94123

Union Square 415-398-7987
500 Sutter Street Mon-Sat 10-5
San Francisco 94102

Presidio Heights 415-923-1454
3314 Sacramento Street Tues-Sat 10:30-5
San Francisco 94118

Thursday's Child ♂

Since 1968 Thursday's Child has been catering to SF's kids (infant to size 14). Tucked in the lower level of a funky old Victorian house, it's been in the biz so long it doesn't bother with minutiae like business cards. The musty place is packed with a mix of handmade clothes and frilly and flowery fashion.

Cow Hollow 415-346-1666
1980 Union Street Mon-Sat 9-6, Sun 10-5
San Francisco 94123

Toujours Fine Lingerie ♀

This peachy jewel box of a shop, the beautiful brainchild of Beverly Weinkauf, is racked with romance and a sweet feminine flair. Find dainty everything from Hanro basics and fine Pluto sleepwear to Gerbe hose and designery lingerie from hard-to-find frilly lines like Edith Eiffel. Weinkauf also offers a special bra-fitting feature for those with challenged chests. www.toujourslingerie.com

Pacific Heights 415-346-3988
2484 Sacramento Street Daily 11-6 (Sun 12-5)
San Francisco 94115 (and by appointment)

True ♂♀

A favorite with the hip-hop herd, this pair of on-the-pulse places houses everything to outfit the young and street-savvy. One entire wall of the women's shop is packed with every kind of backpack, messenger and book bag, balancing the Freshjive footwear and Sergio Valente jeans. For the guys, a few doors along, the submarine-yellow store sells everything from outerwear to underwear, and lines like Phat Farm and Ecko. www.trueclothing.net

Haight-Ashbury (men)   **415-626-2882**
1415 Haight Street   Daily 11-7
San Francisco 94117

Haight-Ashbury (women)   **415-626-2331**
1427 Haight Street   Daily 11-7
San Francisco 94117

TSE

Even without London wonderboy Hussein Chalayan at the helm, you can still count on this sensational sweater out-post for all the cush that comes with cashmere. Among the color-crafted, upscale lollipop looks—twinsets, tops, turtlenecks and cardigans—find soft-edged and smart separates in cashmere and velvet, corduroy, silk or wool blends—all in all, a stylish ready-to-wear collection with feathery-fine accessories.

Union Square   **415-391-1112**
60 Maiden Lane   Mon-Sat 10-6
San Francisco 94108

Peninsula   **650-321-8969**
Stanford Shopping Center   Mon-Fri 10-9, Sat 10-7
Palo Alto 94304   Sun 11-6

Tuffy's Hopscotch

Looking for a fun place to outfit your little one's feet? This colorful kids' shop, teeming with tykes and neighborhood moms, has a fab footwear selection from brands like Pom d'Api, Buckle My Shoe and New Balance. Freshly remod-eled last year, the double space with its hopscotch-painted floorboard also offers a sporty selection of clothes (new-borns to size 12) from Euro faves like Petit Bateau, Lili Gaufrette and Naturino.

Presidio Heights   **415-440-7599**
3307 Sacramento Street   Mon-Sat 10-5:30
San Francisco 94118

Twenty One

Post-collegiate Pac Heights pretties drop in to browse the trendy tops and jeans by Rampage, Bisou Bisou, Max Studio and BCBG. It's not a designer-lover's destination, but with cheap-chic fashions going for $21, $31, and $41 a pop, snagging an outfit for Union Street barhopping does-n't put a dent in the Cosmo cocktail fund.

Cow Hollow   **415-409-2121**
1799 Union Street   Mon-Fri 10:30-7
San Francisco 94123   Sat 10-7, Sun 11-6

UKO

Down on designer duds? Meet David Scott, the owner of this cheery shop on Union Street. He seeks out little-known names who turn out beautiful scarves, shoes and acces-sories. The result is a bits-and-pieces assortment of offbeat contemporary style with a very slight eastern slant.

Cow Hollow   **415-563-0330**
2070 Union Street   Daily 11-6:30 (Sun 12-5:30)
San Francisco 94123

Union Square N.F.L. Sports

Femme fatales steer clear, but sports fans bat a thousand in this shrine to local team uniforms. It's the slam-dunk spot for jerseys, jackets, caps and keepsakes where ladies, gents and even ball-loving babies gear up in 49ers, Giants, Sharks and Warriors garb.

Union Square   **415-291-0484**
184 O'Farrell Street   Daily 10-7
San Francisco 94102

Uomo

Masoud Attar's airy and spiffy Union Square space is nearly as smooth as its large and expertly merchandised selection of men's European sportswear. Downtown's dapper clientele knows casual elegance doesn't come cheaply, but it's no matter once they slip into the private-label leather and ultrasuede sport jackets, vibrant sweaters and sport shirts and Mezlan shoes.

Union Square   **415-989-8666**
475 Sutter Street   Daily 9:30-6:30 (Sun 11-5)
San Francisco 94108

Urban Outfitters

The stomping grounds for the young and the restless, Urban swarms with neo-grunge groupies in search of relaxed rates and up-to-the-nanosecond silhouettes (think terry polos, Diesel denim, muscle tees and colorful hoodies). Mix in a mod housewares corner and you've got a groovy lifestyle space that keeps a music-conscious, baby tee'd, baggy jean'd and budget-bound crowd swinging in style.   www.urbn.com

Union Square   **415-989 1515**
80 Powell Street   Daily 9:30-9:30 (Sun 10:30-9)
San Francisco 94102

Berkeley   **510-486-1300**
2590 Bancroft Way   Daily 10-8 (Sun 12-8)
Berkeley 94704

Valbruna

Named after the town in Italy where owner Marco Tonazzi grew up skiing, this sporty store sells "Italian lifestyle-wear" to its posh Pac Heights clientele. In the winter, stylish skiers and beautiful boarders stock up on Napapijri, Postcard and Vampire before speeding off in their SUVs to the Squaw Valley slopes. In the summer, find warm-weather gear from Nat Naste, Terre and Odlo, outfitting a golf, tennis and sailing crew of the *Wallpaper*-reading sort.   www.valbrunaitaly.com

Pacific Heights   **415-928-3639**
2426 California Street   Daily 11-7
San Francisco 94115   (also by appointment)

☆ Velvet da Vinci

If you're in the market for one-of-a-kind accessories with museum-quality character, Velvet da Vinci is your place. A veritable gallery plush with arty jewelry handcrafted by local and international jewelers and metalsmiths, this funky place is a must-stop for the style savant. Owners Mike Holmes and Elizabeth Shypertt represent 50 artists and host special exhibits frequently, welcoming a revolving roster of new talent. www.velvetdavinci.com

Hayes Valley 415-626-7478
508 Hayes Street Tues-Sat 12-6, Sun 12-4
San Francisco 94102

☆ Ver Unica

Formerly located in a pink Victorian in the Castro, this is a little gem has now moved to a slightly smaller but brighter spot right in the heart of Hayes Valley. Full of handpicked pieces inspected, repaired, cleaned and restored to their original pristine condition, this vintage source flaunts Twenties flapper frocks (head for the back), Forties-through-Sixties cotton day dresses and present-day recycled designer duds to a fashion-conscious crowd. www.ver-unica.com

Hayes Valley 415-431-0688
437b Hayes Street Daily 11-7 (Sun 12-6)
San Francisco 94102

Versace Jeans Couture

For those who carry themselves with confidence, this spunkier (and cheaper) version of Gianni Versace is full of all the wacky prints, glitz and pluck that give the house its sexy, high-energy celebrity. Find the hipped-up Italian Versus collection here (a few doors down from the main Versace store), plus Versace Jeans Couture and all its saucy accessories. www.versace.com

Union Square 415-616-0600
Crocker Galleria Mon-Fri 10-6, Sat 10-5:30
50 Post Street San Francisco 94104

Villains Vault

These rascals have just about seized the Haight Street block between Belvedere and Cole with three Villains outposts, but the stylish subculture set isn't complaining. After all, the retail trio offers something, from shoes to hats, for everyone. Diesel, BCBG max azria, and a serious Levi's selection fill one store; Paul Frank purses, Japanese pop culture T-shirts and trendy streetwear the next; and club-stompers and streetwalkers (Gravis, Giraudon, Diesel) the third.

Haight-Ashbury 415-864-7727
1653 Haight Street Daily 11-7 (winter), 11-8 (summer)
San Francisco 94117

Haight-Ashbury 415-626-5939
1672 Haight Street (opening times as above)
San Francisco 94117

Haight-Ashbury (shoes) **415-626-5939**
1672 Haight Street Daily (opening times as above)
San Francisco 94117

Walkershaw

After 15 years of designing wholesale lines, designer Connie Walkershaw opened her own store to showcase her vintage-inspired collections for women, men and children. Don't miss the matching father and son bowling-style shirts that would make Ricky Ricardo and little Ricky proud. The shop also carries a few items from other lines such as Lola and Miss Fitts plus jewelry by Connie's sister Stefanie Walker.

Haight-Ashbury **415-552-8057**
629 Haight Street Wed-Sat 11-6
San Francisco 94117 Sun 12-5

Walking Co

It doesn't take brain surgery to figure out the philosophy behind this California-based chain. These shoes, sneakers, sandals and boots are made for walking—or strolling, roaming and trekking, for that matter. Find Merrell, Birkenstock, Dansko and Clarks cozy soles, for example, and Walking Co's own line of gardening clogs, loafers, slides and boots. www.walkingco.com

Union Square **415-433-WALK**
228 Powell Street Daily 10-8 (Sun 11-6)
San Francisco 94108

Marin **415-924-5421**
Village at Corte Madera Mon-Fri 10-9, Sat 10-7:30
1554 Redwood Highway Sun 11-6
Corte Madera 94925

The Wasteland

A warehouse of vintage clothing well suited to a counter-culture crowd, Wasteland is stuffed with all the old trappings to retro-fit just about anyone. Broken-in suede and leather, beaten-up denim, wooly cardigans, go-go boots and racks of bowling shirts and bell-bottoms make this SF-based company a popular stop on the secondhand circuit. www.thewasteland.com

Haight-Ashbury **415-863-3150**
1660 Haight Street Mon-Fri 11-7, Sat-Sun 11-8 (winter)
San Francisco 94117 Mon-Sat 11-8, Sun 11-7 (summer)

☆ Waterlilies

If bathing suits are on the shopping agenda, head out to the suburbs for this splashy find. The quiet brick boutique is making waves with its supreme swimwear from designers like Dolce & Gabbana, La Perla, Shan and Malia Mills, and makes trying and buying bikinis a surprisingly pleasant adventure. Also find a bevy of upscale beach accoutrements from pareos to straw and beaded bags. Bank accounts beware, strutting your stuff in Waterlilies wear is no cheap thrill.

Marin   **415-383-2782**
Two El Paseo   Mon-Sat 11-5
Mill Valley 94941

Wavy Footprints ♂

This footwear emporium is one of the only places in Noe Valley to fashion your little ones' feet. They carry a sensational selection of soles (think Doc Martens, Elefanten, Skechers, Vans, Teva and Buckle My Shoe) among slippers, socks, backpacks, raingear and hair accessories.   www.wavyfootprints.com

Noe Valley   **415-285-3668**
3961 24th Street   Daily 10-6
San Francisco 94114

Weston Wear ♀

Those sexy, stretchy kaleidoscopic shirts that designer Julienne Weston has been cutting since 1981 are on sale (10-25% off retail) at this tiny store. Production overruns and samples of the trendy dance-inspired wear—from tops to skirts—are stuffed into this secret spot that has Weston Wear junkies jetting to the Mission.   www.westonwear.com

Mission   **415-695-2869**
3491 19th Street   Daily 12-6
San Francisco 94110

Wet Seal ♀

Junior trend-junkies feed off the affordable and ultra-fad fashion from this Southern California-based chain. From the folks who are also responsible for Arden B. and Zutopia you'll find fun and funky jeans, tight-fitting tees, undies, pjs and accessories—perfect picks to take a teen from day to night.   www.wetseal.com

Sunset   **415-564-0908**
Stonestown Galleria   Daily 10-9 (Sun 11-6)
3251 20th Avenue   San Francisco 94132

Union Square   **415-541-0983**
San Francisco Shopping Centre   Mon-Sat 9:30-8
865 Market Street   Sun 11-6
San Francisco 94103

Wilkes Bashford ♂♀

Never mind the apparently snooty sales staff at this quintes-sential San Francisco specialty shop…the atmosphere may be a bit stuffy but the stuff is top-notch. Wilkes, an SF personali-ty who's been dressing the social set and prominent politicos, including Mayor Willie Brown, since 1966, champions the fashion champs (think Dolce & Gabbana, Brioni, Bogner, Yohji and Gaultier). From menswear classics to tailored goods for the gals and a hint of housewares from Sue Fisher King, the stock in this six-floor, mini-department store is sure to seduce any stylish stuffed shirt.   www.wilkesbashford.com

Union Square   **415-986-4380**
375 Sutter Street   Mon-Sat 10-6 (Thurs 10-8)
San Francisco 94108

The Peninsula   650-322-7080
Stanford Shopping Center   Mon-Fri 10-9, Sat 11-7
Palo Alto 94304   Sun 11-6

WilkesSport

The more casually clad can pick up their sophisticated weekend threads at this easygoing arm of Wilkes Bashford. Situated in a Bay Area burb, this specialty store keeps a well-to-do crew clothed in conservative fashions from the likes of Zegna Sport, Etro and Loro Piana. Find shoes, bags and determined sales clerks.   www.wilkessport.com

Marin   415-381-5183
57 Throckmorton Avenue   Daily 10-7 (Sun 11-6)
Mill Valley 94941

Wilsons Leather

For a quick pick-me-up duck into this Minnesota-based mall classic for a little something in leather. Hides of all hues and forms make up the merchandise (10,200 styles) at this no-frills shop. Look for gloves, backpacks, briefcases, cell phone cases, wallets and, best of all, apparel—from boot-cut jeans to classic blazers and form-fitting jackets. Large sizes also available.   www.wilsonsleather.com

Union Square   415-434-0777
764 Market Street   Daily 10-7 (Sun 11-6)
San Francisco 94102

Wolford

The world of wonderful Wolford started with ultra-luxe leg-wear; now it's an entire universe of high-end, high-tech and high-ticket items. Among the velvety tights, opaque amaze-ments and silky, slenderizing stockings find men's ribbed socks, must-have bodysuits and super-supple swimwear. Look for the Austrian's new Logic line, a waistband-less Lycra hose with the densest of weaves.   www.wolford.com

Union Square   415-391-6727
115 Maiden Lane   Mon-Sat 10-6
San Francisco 94108

☆ Workshop

This Union Street fixture is a clothes hound's haven, where owner Susan Kim seeks out eclectic femme-wear—sweet and exotic finds like Dosa's slipdresses and camisoles, Easton Pearson embellished attire and Emma Hope shoes. Be sure not to miss the luxe Lingerie Cottage, Kim's quaint little Victorian out back, a shrine to sumptuous silks, stock-ings, slips and swimwear.

Cow Hollow   415-561-9551
2254 Union Street   Mon-Sat 10-6
San Francisco 94123

Workwear

The men's merch from parent company Cotton Basics is found in this pared-down boutique. All the company's col-orful cotton T-shirts for the boys are sold here, along with

Carhartt shorts, Liberty overalls, pants and jackets and a rack of Dickies overalls. Call it farmer fashion, or just a decent dose of uniform-like essentials. Find a small selection for women, too.

Noe Valley   **415-206-0245**
3989 24th Street   Daily 11-7 (Sun 11-6)
San Francisco 94114

Worn Out West
In the heart of the Castro, WOW houses everything, well, worn out west. A blend of new and used garments, the store has everything for a cowpoke's closet—Levi's, flannels and cowboy boots, which are all secondhand. Love a man in a uniform? This place also dabbles in naval, police, military and security wear, plus a gang of motorcycle gear and leather jackets including Worn Out West's own high-end line.

Castro   **415-431-6020**
582 Castro Street   Daily 12-7 (Sat 11-7)
San Francisco 94114

X Generation
These three neighboring stores under the same ownership (although one's called Dirty Jeans) feed teeny-bob trends to throngs of tourists and city kids who appreciate seasonally disposable duds at palatable prices. Styles are sheer and skimpy, lacy and liberated, perfectly tight fits for the taut teen.

Haight-Ashbury   **415-255-2838**
1606 Haight Street   Daily 11-7 (Sun 12-6)
San Francisco 94117

Haight-Ashbury   **415-863-6040**
1401 Haight Street   (opening times as above)
San Francisco 94117

Haight-Ashbury   **415-355-9022**
1641 Haight Street   (opening times as above)
San Francisco 94117

Yak Pak Store
Yak Pak's SF arrival was a score for the young urban set. The sturdy nylon bags from Brooklyn are a booming commodity in these parts, the messenger bag gone mod. The merch here covers every square inch (even the bathroom is decked with Yak Pak Apt's line of home accessories)—Dickies, Levi's, Coleman (all Yak Pak licensees), as well as their own signature brand. Find record bags, knapsacks and laptop cases among other bizarre bag styles.   www.yakpak.com

Haight-Ashbury   **415-241-0885**
1474 Haight Street   Daily 11-7
San Francisco 94117

Yountville
A yupscale mommy's favorite source for the haute and happening. The cheery shop is chock-full of tiny and trendy bits

like cashmere sweaters, silk blouses and jeans from Euro favorites like Miniman. Dish it out for other designers including Malina, Catamini and Cozy Toes, and pint-size suits, pajamas, shoes and chichi tchotchkes.

Pacific Heights 415-922-5050
2416 Fillmore Street Daily 11-5:30 (Sun 11-4)
San Francisco 94115

Yoya Boutique

Former software designer turned fashion maven, Phoebe Jacobson says "anybody can spend a lot of money and get great clothes, what's more challenging is to find stylish fashions that have good value." Her shop exemplifies this attitude with reasonably priced finds from French, Italian and American lines like Morgan de Toi, Tara Jarmon, Betty Blue, Celyn b. and KLD Signature. Noe Valley gals are happy to have a little Union Street style at lower prices, right in their own neighborhood. www.yoyaboutique.com

Noe Valley 415-550-6788
4028b 24th Street Daily 11-7 (Sun 11-6)
San Francisco 94114

Yves Saint Laurent

Since its February 2002 opening YSL's been a Maiden Lane haute stop for Tom Ford's women's and men's Rive Gauche line as well as accessories and fragrances. Step down the entrance steps and into an atmosphere of black lacquer walls and raw concrete floors that's just a little slicker than the serious staff.

Union Square 415-837-1211
166 Maiden Lane Daily 10-6 (Sun 12-5)
San Francisco 94108

Zeni

This small specialty boutique keeps the somewhat stylish but equally offbeat Hayes Valley crowd in funky, flirty and smart fashion. Among Zeni's own line of young contemporary sweater jackets, reversible tops and dresses, find lines like Nicole Miller and Anna Sui for women, and Frederichomsownwear and BCBG max azria for men. There's also a small selection of men's underwear, Smith sunglasses and snazzy sacs from Angela Amiri.

Hayes Valley 415-864-0154
567 Hayes Street Mon-Tues 12-6, Wed-Fri 12-7
San Francisco 94102 Sat 11-7, Sun 11-6

Stores by Neighborhood

San Francisco Area Map

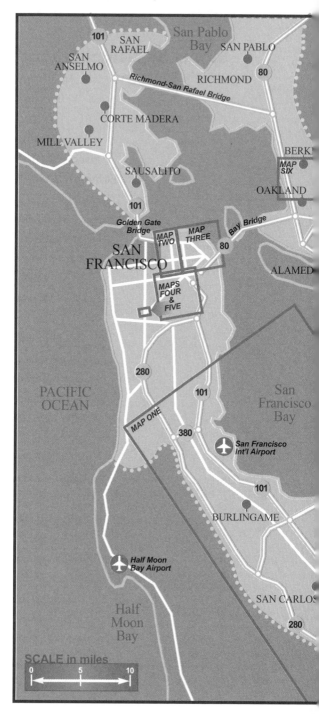

San Francisco Area Map

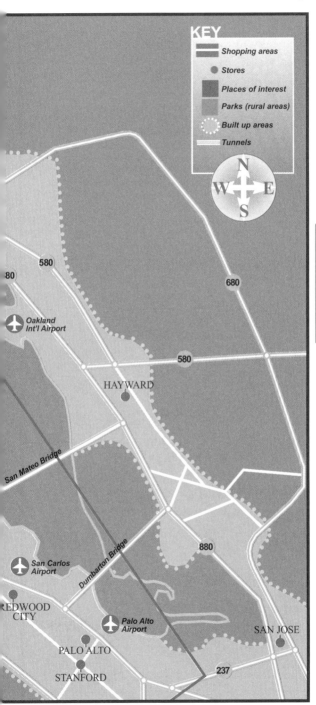

Peninsula

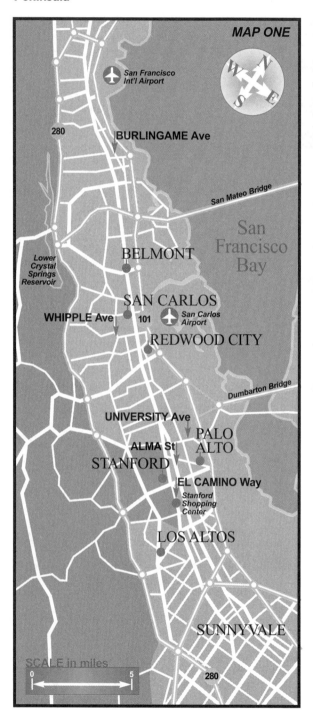

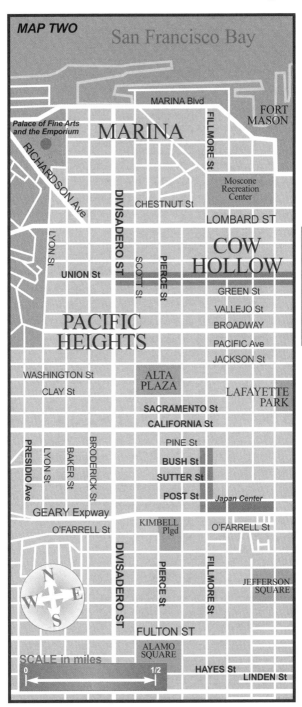

MAP TWO

San Francisco Bay

MARINA Blvd

FORT MASON

FILLMORE St

Palace of Fine Arts and the Emporium

MARINA

RICHARDSON Ave

Moscone Recreation Center

DIVISADERO ST

CHESTNUT St

LOMBARD ST

LYON St

SCOTT St

PIERCE St

COW HOLLOW

UNION St

GREEN St

VALLEJO St

BROADWAY

PACIFIC HEIGHTS

PACIFIC Ave

JACKSON St

WASHINGTON St

CLAY St

ALTA PLAZA

LAFAYETTE PARK

SACRAMENTO St

CALIFORNIA St

PINE St

BUSH St

PRESIDIO Ave

LYON St

BAKER St

BRODERICK St

SUTTER St

POST St

Japan Center

GEARY Expway

O'FARRELL St

KIMBELL Plgd

O'FARRELL St

DIVISADERO ST

PIERCE St

FILLMORE St

JEFFERSON SQUARE

N
W E
S

FULTON ST

SCALE in miles

0   1/2

ALAMO SQUARE

HAYES St

LINDEN St

Neighborhoods

Union Square

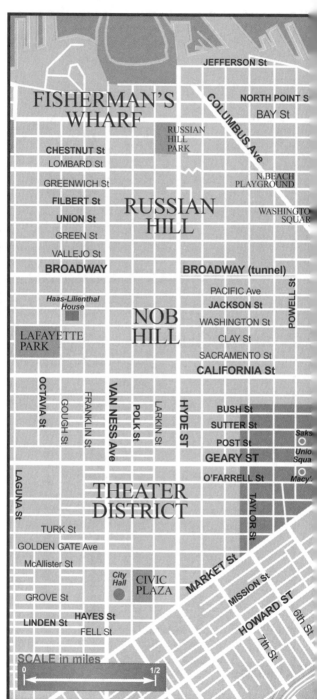

Union Square

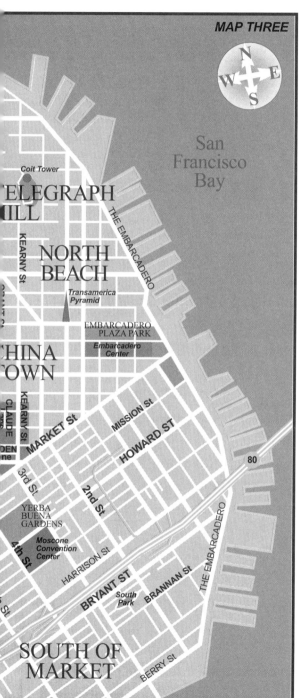

Castro / Mission

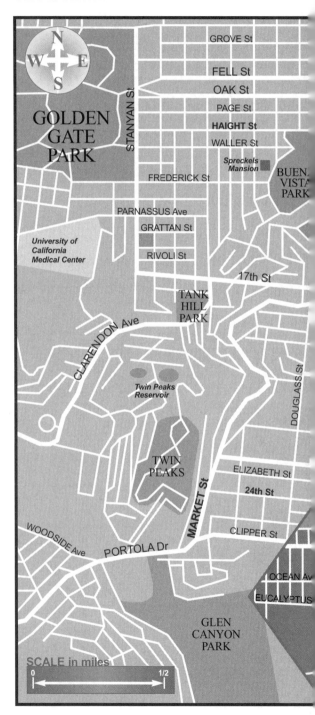

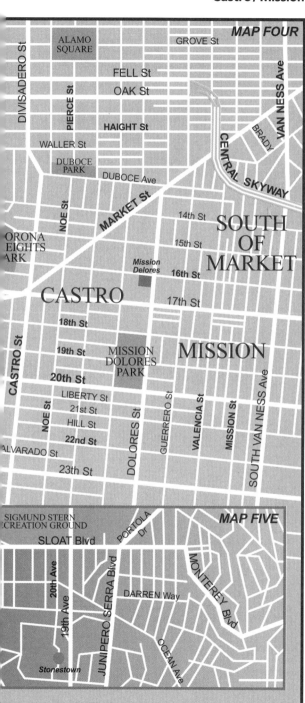

Berkeley

Berkeley

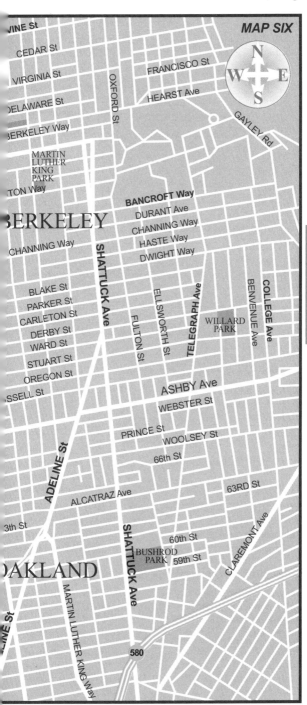

Neighborhoods

Berkeley *See map pages 114–115*

Any Mountain	2777 Shattuck Avenue
Body Options	3212 College Avenue
Buffalo Exchange	2585 Telegraph Avenue
Clobba	2570 Bancroft Way
Cotton Basics	2907 College Avenue
Dharma	2391 Telegraph Avenue
Dharma	2116 Vine Street
Dish	2981 College Avenue
Erica Tanov	1827 4th Street
Express	2576 Bancroft Way
Foot Locker	2307 Telegraph Avenue
Gap	2310 Telegraph Avenue
Jeremys	2967 College Avenue
Jest Jewels	1791 4th Street
Margaret O'Leary	1832 4th Street
Marmot Mountain Works	3049 Adeline Street
Mars Mercantile	2398 Telegraph Avenue
The North Face	1238 5th Street
Ovation	3206 College Avenue
Rabat	1825 4th Street
REI	1338 San Pablo Avenue
Riki	2111 Vine Street
This Little Piggy Wears Cotton	1840 4th Street
Urban Outfitters	2590 Bancroft Way

Castro *See map pages 112–113*

All American Boy	463 Castro Street
Body Body Wear	535 Castro Street
Body/Citizen	4071 18th Street
Citizen	536 Castro Street
Clobba	587 Castro Street
Crossroads Trading Company	2231 Market Street
Gap	1975 Market Street
IN-JEAN-IOUS	432 Castro Street
Rolo 450	450 Castro Street
Rolo on Market	2351 Market Street
Rolo Undercover	545 Castro Street
Worn Out West	582 Castro Street

Cow Hollow *See map page 109*

1887 Dance Shoppe	2206 Union Street
A/X Armani Exchange	2090 Union Street
Abigail Morgan	1640 Union Street
Ambiance	1864 Union Street
Azadeh	2066 Union Street
bebe	2095 Union Street
Body Options	2100 Union Street
Boutique Here	2116 Union Street

Bryan Lee	1840 Union Street
By Emily	2271 Union Street
Canyon Beachwear	1728 Union Street
Cara Mia	1814 Union Street
Carol Doda's Champagne & Lace Lingerie Boutique	1850 Union Street
Dantone	1796 Union Street
Erin Paige	1849 Union Street
Fenzi Uomo	1801 Union Street
Fog City Leather	2060 Union Street
Georgiou	1725 Union Street
Girlfriends Beverly Hills	1824 Union Street
House of Cashmere	2674 Octavia Street
Jennifer Croll/Croll Sport	1810 Union Street
Jest Jewels	1869 Union Street
Kenneth Cole	2078 Union Street
Lorenzini	2149 Union Street
MetroSport	2198 Filbert Street
Minis	2278 Union Street
Mona Lisa	2277 Union Street
Mudpie	1694 Union Street
Nida	2163 Union Street
Nine West	2086 Union Street
Oceana Rain	3024 Fillmore Street
Peluche	1954 Union Street
Riley James	3027 Fillmore Street
Rin	2111 Union Street
Sean	1749 Union Street
Shaw Shoes	2001 Union Street
Smith Williams	1827 Union Street
Sugar Shack	1858 Union Street
Three Bags Full	2181 Union Street
Thursday's Child	1980 Union Street
Twenty One	1799 Union Street
UKO	2070 Union Street
Workshop	2254 Union Street

Financial District *See map page 111*

Ann Taylor	3 Embarcadero Center
Banana Republic	2 Embarcadero Center
Cable Car Clothiers	200 Bush Street
Enzo Angiolini	1 Embarcadero Center
Gap	3 Embarcadero Center
Gap Kids & Baby Gap	3 Embarcadero Center
Georgiou	3 Embarcadero Center
Jest Jewels	3 Embarcadero Center
Liz Claiborne	4 Embarcadero Center
Nine West	4 Embarcadero Center

Neighborhoods

Fisherman's Wharf *See map page 110*

Gap	1 Jefferson Street
Gap Kids & Baby Gap	1 Jefferson Street
Patagonia	770 North Point

Ghirardelli Square

Ann Taylor	900 North Point Street

Glen Park

Romantasy Exquisite Corsetry	2912 Diamond Street

Haight-Ashbury *See map pages 112–113*

Aaardvarks	1501 Haight Street
Ambiance	1458 Haight Street
Behind the Post Office	1510 Haight Street
Buffalo Exchange	1555 Haight Street
Cal Surplus	1541 Haight Street
Clobba	1604 Haight Street
Crossroads Trading Company	1519 Haight Street
Daljeets	1773 Haight Street
Dharma	1600 Haight Street
Duzz 1020	1780 Haight Street
Gap	1485 Haight Street
Happy Trails	1615 Haight Street
Held Over	1543 Haight Street
House of Flys	1605 Haight Street
Hoy's Sports	1632 Haight Street
Joe Pye	351 Divisadero Street
John Fluevog Shoes	1697 Haight Street
Kids Only	1608 Haight Street
Kweejibo Clothing Company	1580 Haight Street
La Rosa	1711 Haight Street
Lost Horizon	1506 Haight Street
Luichiny	1529 Haight Street
Piedmont	1452 Haight Street
Positively Haight Street	1400 Haight Street
Redfive	1472 Haight Street
Satellite Vintage	1364 Haight Street
ShoeBiz	1422 Haight Street
ShoeBiz	1446 Haight Street
ShoeBiz	1553 Haight Street
Sparky's Vintage Clothing	1764 Haight Street
Stüssy	1409 Haight Street
Sugarpussy	248 Fillmore Street
Sunhee Moon	142 Fillmore Street
True	1415 Haight Street
True	1427 Haight Street
Villains Vault	1653 Haight Street

Villains Vault	1672 Haight Street
Walkershaw	629 Haight Street
The Wasteland	1660 Haight Street
X Generation	1401 Haight Street
X Generation	1606 Haight Street
X Generation	1641 Haight Street
Yak Pak Store	1474 Haight Street

Hayes Valley *See map page 109*

Alla Prima	539 Hayes Street
Bulo	418 Hayes Street
Bulo	437a Hayes Street
Buu	506 Hayes Street
Coquette	564 Hayes Street
Dark Garden	321 Linden Street
Flight 001	525 Hayes Street
Gimme Shoes	416 Hayes Street
Haseena	526 Hayes Street
Lava 9	542 Hayes Street
Manifesto:	514 Octavia Street
Minnie Wilde	519 Laguna Street
Nida	544 Hayes Street
Nomads	556 Hayes Street
Paolo	524 Hayes Street
She	528 Hayes Street
Velvet da Vinci	508 Hayes Street
Ver Unica	437b Hayes Street
Zeni	567 Hayes Street

Marin

Alençon Couture Bridal	318 Miller Avenue, Mill Valley
Ann Taylor Loft	100 Corte Madera Town Center Corte Madera
Any Mountain	71 Tamal Vista Boulevard, Mill Valley
Banana Republic	59 Throckmorton Avenue, Mill Valley
Banana Republic	Village at Corte Madera
Bebe	Village at Corte Madera
Canyon Beachwear	634 San Anselmo Avenue San Anselmo
Chadwicks of London	9 Throckmorton Avenue, Mill Valley
Chadwicks of London	526 San Anselmo Avenue San Anselmo
Chico's	Village at Corte Madera
Coach	Village at Corte Madera
CP Shades	Strawberry Village, Mill Valley
Express	Village at Corte Madera
Foot Locker	Village at Corte Madera
Gap	Village at Corte Madera

Neighborhoods

Gap Kids & Baby Gap	Village at Corte Madera
GapBody	Village at Corte Madera
Gene Hiller	729 Bridgeway, Sausalito
Georgiou	579 Bridgeway, Sausalito
Gingiss Formal Wear	8950 Northgate Mall, San Rafael
J.Crew	Village at Corte Madera
J.Jill	Village at Corte Madera
Lady Foot Locker	Village at Corte Madera
Lucky Brand	Village at Corte Madera
Macy's	Village at Corte Madera
Margaret O'Leary	14 Miller Avenue, Mill Valley
Marshalls	313 Corte Madera Town Center
Mill Valley Hat Box	118 Throckmorton Avenue Mill Valley
Mimi Maternity	Village at Corte Madera
Nine West	Village at Corte Madera
Nordstrom	Village at Corte Madera
REI	213 Corte Madera Town Center
Ross Dress for Less	194 Donahue Street, Marin City
Selix	874 4th Street, San Rafael
Talbots	Village at Corte Madera
Walking Co	Village at Corte Madera
Waterlilies	Two El Paseo, Mill Valley
WilkesSport	57 Throckmorton Avenue, Mill Valley

Marina *See map page 109*

AMA	2276 Chestnut Street
Body Options	2108 Chestnut Street
Catnip & Bones	2220 Chestnut Street
Chadwicks of London	2068 Chestnut Street
City Fitness	3251 Pierce Street
dress	2258 Chestnut Street
dress	2271 Chestnut Street
Fleet Feet Sports	2076 Chestnut Street
Gap	2159 Chestnut Street
Gap Kids & Baby Gap	2159 Chestnut Street
GapBody	2040 Chestnut Street
Jorja	2015 Chestnut Street
Lucky Brand	2301 Chestnut Street
The News	2260 Chestnut Street
Ovation	2124 Chestnut Street
Rabat	2080 Chestnut Street
Shoesizes	2798 Lombard Street
Smash Footwear	2030 Chestnut Street
Studio On Chestnut	2233 Chestnut Street

Mission *See map pages 112–113*

Alternative Design Studio	3458 18th Street
Bombay Bazaar/Bombay Sari Palace	548 Valencia Street

Dema	1038 Valencia Street
Dharma	914 Valencia Street
Foot Locker	2829 Mission Street
Gap	1975 Market Street
hrm Boutique	924 Valencia Street
Kweejibo Clothing Company	541 Valencia Street
Laku	1069 Valencia Street
Retro Fit Vintage	910 Valencia Street
Ruby Gallery	3602 20th Street
Schauplatz	791 Valencia Street
Skechers USA	2600 Mission Street
Subterrancan Shoe Room	877 Valencia Street
Therapy	545 Valencia Street
Therapy	758 Valencia Street
Weston Wear	3491 19th Street

Nob Hill *See map page 110*

American Rag Cie	1305 Van Ness Avenue
Buffalo Exchange	1800 Polk Street
Girl Stuff	2255 Polk Street
Lombardi Sports	1600 Jackson Street
Ross Dress for Less	1645 Van Ness Avenue
Sugar Poppy	1552 Polk Street

Noe Valley

A Girl and her Dog	3932 24th Street
Ambiance	3985 24th Street
Astrid's Rabat Shoes & Accessories	3909 24th Street
Cotton Basics	1301 Castro Street
Designer's Club	3899 24th Street
Guys & Dolls Vintage	3789 24th Street
Ocean Front Walkers	4069 24th Street
Rabat	4001 24th Street
Riki	4037 24th Street
See Jane Run	3870 24th Street
Small Frys	4066 24th Street
Wavy Footprints	3961 24th Street
Workwear	3989 24th Street
Yoya Boutique	4028b 24th Street

North Beach *See map page 111*

Ab Fits	1519 Grant Avenue
Alla Prima	1420 Grant Avenue
Babette	1400 Grant Avenue
Fife	1450 Grant Avenue
Knitz & Leather	1429 Grant Avenue
Lilith	1528 Grant Avenue
MAC	1543 Grant Avenue
Martha Egan	1 Columbus Avenue

Neighborhoods

| Old Vogue | 1412 Grant Avenue |
| Ooma | 1422 Grant Avenue |

Oakland *See map pages 114–115*

Birkenstock SF	6012 College Avenue
Body Options	2056 Mountain Boulevard
Cotton Basics	5540 College Avenue
Crossroads Trading Company	5636 College Avenue

Foot Locker	1 Eastmont Mall
Foot Locker	3275 Lakeshore Avenue
See Jane Run	5817 College Avenue
Selix	1724 Broadway

Pacific Heights *See map page 109*

Annies	2512 Sacramento Street
Baxter Hull	1906 Fillmore Street
bebe	2133 Fillmore Street
Betsey Johnson	2031 Fillmore Street

Blu	2259 Fillmore Street
Body Options	2216 Fillmore Street
Brown Eyed Girl	2999 Washington Street
Bulo	3044 Fillmore Street

Cielo	2225 Fillmore Street
Crossroads Trading Company	1901 Fillmore Street
Crosswalk Specialty Shoes	2122 Fillmore Street
DEPARTURES, from the Past	2028 Fillmore Street

Gimme Shoes	2358 Fillmore Street
Harputs	1527 Fillmore Street
Heather	2408 Fillmore Street
Heidi Says	2426 Fillmore Street

jim-elle	2237 Fillmore Street
Joan Gilbert Bridal Collection	
L'Uomo International	2121 Fillmore Street
Margaret O'Leary	2400 Fillmore Street

Mio	2035 Fillmore Street
Mrs Dewson's Hats	2050 Fillmore Street
My Boudoir	2029 Fillmore Street
Paolo	1971 Sutter Street

Sarah Shaw	3095 Sacramento Street
Toujours Fine Lingerie	2484 Sacramento Street
Valbruna	2426 California Street
Yountville	2416 Fillmore Street

Peninsula *See map page 108*

A/X Armani Exchange	Stanford Shopping Center
Any Mountain	928 Whipple Avenue, Redwood City
Barcelino	Stanford Shopping Center

| Bebe | Stanford Shopping Center |
| Benetton | Stanford Shopping Center |

Bloomingdale's	Stanford Shopping Center
Brooks Brothers	Stanford Shopping Center
Chico's	1113 Burlingame Avenue, Burlingame
Chico's	396 University Avenue, Palo Alto
Cielo	Stanford Shopping Center
Coach	Stanford Shopping Center
Eddie Bauer	Stanford Shopping Center
Foot Locker	3225 El Camino Real
Foot Locker	320 University Avenue, Palo Alto
Gap	Stanford Shopping Center
Gap Kids & Baby Gap	Stanford Shopping Center
Georgiou	Stanford Shopping Center
The Grocery Store	311 Primrose Road, Burlingame
J.Crew	Stanford Shopping Center
Jennifer Croll/Croll Sport	34 North Santa Cruz, Los Gatos
Kenneth Cole	Stanford Shopping Center
Lady Foot Locker	Stanford Shopping Center
L'Uomo International	Stanford Shopping Center
Macy's	Stanford Shopping Center
MaxMara	Stanford Shopping Center
MetroSport	37 Town & Country Village
Neiman Marcus	Stanford Shopping Center
Nine West	Stanford Shopping Center
Nordstrom	Stanford Shopping Center
The North Face	217 Alma Street, Palo Alto
Oilily	Stanford Shopping Center
Peluche	348 Lorton Avenue, Burlingame
Ralph Lauren	Stanford Shopping Center
Susan	1403 Burlingame Avenue, Burlingame
Talbots	Stanford Shopping Center
TSE	Stanford Shopping Center
Wilkes Bashford	Stanford Shopping Center

Potrero Hill

Gap	2300 16th Street
Gap Kids & Baby Gap	2300 16th Street
Old Navy	2300 16th Street

Presidio Heights

The Bar	340 Presidio Avenue
Bettina	3654 Sacramento Street
Button Down	3415 Sacramento Street
Dean Hutchinson	3401 Sacramento Street
The Designer Consigner	3525 Sacramento Street
Dialogue	3375 Sacramento Street
Dialogue Sport	3376 Sacramento Street
Dottie Doolittle	3680 Sacramento Street
emily lee	3509 California Street
Fetish	344 Presidio Avenue

Neighborhoods

Gap Kids & Baby Gap	3491 California Street
Good Byes	3464 Sacramento Street
Good Byes	3483 Sacramento Street
Grace Couture	3600 Sacramento Street
The Grocery Store	3625 Sacramento Street
Jonathan Kaye Baby	3615 Sacramento Street
The Junior Boot Shop	3555 California Street
KinderSport	3566 Sacramento Street
Maison De Belles Choses	3263 Sacramento Street
Mom's the Word	3385 Sacramento Street
Susan	3685 Sacramento Street
Three Bags Full	3314 Sacramento Street
Tuffy's Hopscotch	3307 Sacramento Street

Richmond

April in Paris	55 Clement Street
Gap	4228 Geary Boulevard
Ross Dress for Less	5200 Geary Boulevard

Russian Hill *See map page 110*

Atelier des Modistes	1903 Hyde Street
Cris	2056 Polk Street

SoMa *See map pages 111 & 113*

A Motion Studio	440 Brannan Street
Babette	92 South Park
Burlington Coat Factory	899 Howard Street
Georgiou	925 Bryant Street
Golden Bear Sportswear	200 Potrero Street
Harper Greer	580 4th Street
ISDA & Co Outlet	29 South Park
Jeremys	2 South Park
Rolo Garage	1301 Howard Street
Rolo SoMa	1235 Howard Street
Stormy Leather	1158 Howard Street

South San Francisco

Jessica McClintock	494 Forbes Boulevard

Sunset/Stonestown Galleria

Abercrombie & Fitch	3251 20th Avenue
Alaya	1256 9th Avenue
Aldo	3251 20th Avenue
Ann Taylor	3251 20th Avenue
Banana Republic	3251 20th Avenue
bebe	3251 20th Avenue
Body Options	3251 20th Avenue
Chico's	3251 20th Avenue
Eddie Bauer	3251 20th Avenue

Enzo Angiolini	3251 20th Avenue
Express	3251 20th Avenue
Foot Locker	3251 20th Avenue
Gap	3251 20th Avenue
Gap Kids & Baby Gap	3251 20th Avenue
Gingiss Formal Wear	3251 20th Avenue
Guess?	3251 20th Avenue
J.Crew	3251 20th Avenue
Luba	751 Irving Street
Macy's	3251 20th Avenue
Nine West	3251 20th Avenue
Nordstrom	285 Winston Drive
On the Run	1310 9th Avenue
Selix	2622 Ocean Avenue
Talbots	3251 20th Avenue
Wet Seal	3251 20th Avenue

Tenderloin

Any Mountain	2598 Taylor Street

Union Square   *See map pages 110–111*

A Pea in the Pod	290 Sutter Street
Abercrombie & Fitch	865 Market Street
Aerosoles	414 Sutter Street
agnès b.	33 Grant Avenue
The Alden Shop	201 Kearny Street
Aldo	844 Market Street
Alfred Dunhill	250 Post Street
Allen Edmonds	171 Post Street
American Eagle Outfitters	865 Market Street
Ann Taylor	865 Market Street
Ann Taylor	240 Post Street
Ann Taylor Loft	246 Sutter Street
Anthropologie	880 Market Street
Arden B.	865 Market Street
Aricie	50 Post Street
Arthur Beren Shoes	222 Stockton Street
Banana Republic	256 Grant Avenue
Barcelino	50 Post Street
Barcelino	476 Post Street
Barcelino	498 Post Street
BCBG max azria	331 Powell Street
BCBG max azria	865 Market Street
bebe	21 Grant Avenue
bebe	865 Market Street
Benetton	865 Market Street
Benetton	39 Stockton Street
Betsey Johnson	160 Geary Street
BillyBlue	54 Geary Street

Neighborhoods

Birkenstock SF	42 Stockton Street
Bottega Veneta	108 Geary Street
Brooks Brothers	150 Post Street
Burberry	225 Post Street
Camper	33 Grant Avenue
Casual Corner	301 Geary Street
Chanel	155 Maiden Lane
Charles David	865 Market Street
Chico's	865 Market Street
The Children's Place	180 Sutter Street
Christian Dior	216 Stockton Street
Cicada	547 Sutter Street
Cicada	555 Sutter Street, 4th floor
Club Monaco	865 Market Street
Coach	190 Post Street
Coach	865 Market Street
Cole Haan	324 Stockton Street
Courtoué	459-465 Geary Street
Couture	395 Sutter Street
David Stephen	50 Maiden Lane
Diana Slavin	3 Claude Lane
Diesel	101 Post Street
The Disney Store	400 Post Street
Don Sherwood Golf & Tennis World	320 Grant Avenue
Dreamweaver	171 Maiden Lane
DSW Shoe Warehouse	111 Powell Street
ecco	236 Post Street
Eddie Bauer	250 Post Street
Emporio Armani	1 Grant Avenue
Enzo Angiolini	865 Market Street
Escada	259 Post Street
Express	865 Market Street
fil à fil	50 Post Street
Fitelle	865 Market Street
Foot Locker	865 Market Street
Fossil	55 Stockton Street
French Connection	101 Powell Street
Frette	124 Geary Street
Gap	890 Market Street
Gap	100 Post Street
Gap Kids & Baby Gap	890 Market Street
Gap Kids & Baby Gap	100 Post Street
GapBody	890 Market Street
Georgiou	152 Geary Street
Ghurka	170 Post Street
Gianni Versace	60 Post Street
Ginger's Bridal Salon	130 Maiden Lane
Gimme Shoes	50 Grant Avenue
Gingiss Formal Wear	170 Sutter Street

Giorgio Armani	278 Post Street
Gucci	200 Stockton Street
Guess?	90 Grant Avenue
Guess?	865 Market Street
Henry Cotton's	105 Grant Avenue
Hermès	125 Grant Avenue
The Hound	140 Sutter Street
House of Blue Jeans	979 Market Street
J.Crew	865 Market Street
J.Jill	865 Market Street
Jaeger	272 Post Street
Japanese Weckend Maternity	500 Sutter Street
Jessica McClintock	180 Geary Street
Jin Wang	111 Maiden Lane
Joanie Char	527 Sutter Street
Johnston & Murphy	299 Post Street
Kate Spade	227 Grant Avenue
Kati Koós	500 Sutter Street
Kenneth Cole	166 Grant Avenue
Kenneth Cole	865 Market Street
La Maison de la Bouquetière	563 Sutter Street
Lady Foot Locker	865 Market Street
Levi Strauss	300 Post Street
Lily Samii Collection	260 Stockton Street
Loehmann's	222 Sutter Street
Louis Vuitton	233 Geary Street
Lucky Brand	865 Market Street
MAC	5 Claude Lane
Macy's	170 O'Farrell Street
Marc Jacobs	125 Maiden Lane
Margaret O'Leary	One Claude Lane
Marina Morrison	30 Maiden Lane
Marshalls	901 Market Street
MaxMara	175 Post Street
Max Nugus Haute Couture	537 Sutter Street
The Men's Wearhouse	17 Stockton Street
Metier	355 Sutter Street
Mix	309 Sutter Street
Neiman Marcus	150 Stockton Street
New Balance	222 Sutter Street
Niketown	278 Post Street
Nine West	865 Market Street
Nine West	250 Stockton Street
Nordstrom	865 Market Street
North Beach Leather	224 Grant Avenue
The North Face	180 Post Street
Old Navy	801 Market Street
Paul Frank	262 Sutter Street
Prada	140 Geary Street
Puma	856 Market Street

Neighborhoods

The Rafaels	643 Market Street
The Rafaels	285 Geary Street
Ralph Lauren	90 Post Street
Reva Mivasagar: The Guild	375 Grant Avenue
Ria Shoes	301 Grant Avenue
Ria Shoes	437 Sutter Street
Rockport	165 Post Street
Ross Dress for Less	799 Market Street
The Sak	334 Grant Avenue
Saks Fifth Avenue	384 Post Street
Saks Men's Store	220 Post Street
Salvatore Ferragamo	233 Geary Street
Scheuer Linens	340 Sutter Street
Selix	123 Kearny Street
Sisley	59 Grant Avenue
Skechers USA	770 Market Street
Steve Madden	865 Market Street
St. John	767 Market Street
Talbots	128 Post Street
Thomas Pink	255 Post Street
Three Bags Full	500 Sutter Street
TSE	60 Maiden Lane
Union Square N.F.L. Sports	184 O'Farrell Street
Uomo	475 Sutter Street
Urban Outfitters	80 Powell Street
Versace Jeans Couture	50 Post Street
Walking Co	228 Powell Street
Wet Seal	865 Market Street
Wilkes Bashford	375 Sutter Street
Wilsons Leather	764 Market Street
Wolford	115 Maiden Lane
Yves Saint Laurent	166 Maiden Lane

Western Addition

Third Hand Store	1839 Divisadero Street

Stores by Category

Women's

Men's

Unisex

Children's

Women's Accessories

Abigail Morgan
Alaya
AMA
Annies

Anthropologie
Banana Republic
Baxter Hull
Bloomingdale's

Coach
Dialogue Sport
emily lee
Fetish

Flight 001
Girl Stuff
The Grocery Store
Hermès

Jest Jewels
Joe Pye
Kate Spade
Laku

Lava 9
Macy's
Metier
Neiman Marcus

Net-a-Porter
Nordstrom
Ooma
Piedmont

Riley James
Rin
Ruby Gallery
Saks Fifth Avenue

Sarah Shaw
St. John
Sugar Poppy
Susan

True
Velvet da Vinci
Wilkes Bashford
Yak Pak Store

Women's Bridal

Alençon Couture Bridal
Atelier des Modistes
By Emily

Cicada
Ginger's Bridal Salon
Grace Couture
Jessica McClintock

Jin Wang
Joan Gilbert Bridal
  Collection

Marina Morrison
Reva Mivasagar: The Guild
Third Hand Store

Women's Career

Ann Taylor
Bloomingdale's
Brooks Brothers

Casual Corner
Georgiou
Jaeger
Liz Claiborne

Macy's
Neiman Marcus
Nordstrom

Saks Fifth Avenue
St. John
Talbots

Women's Cashmere/Knitwear

Dreamweaver
House of Cashmere
Knitz & Leather

Margaret O'Leary
Three Bags Full
TSE

Women's Casual

A/X Armani Exchange
Abercrombie & Fitch
Alaya
American Eagle Outfitters

Ann Taylor Loft
Anthropologie
Banana Republic
Baxter Hull

Benetton
Bloomingdale's
Brooks Brothers
Casual Corner

Chico's
City Fitness
Club Monaco
Cotton Basics

CP Shades
Daljeets
Dharma
Dialogue

Dialogue Sport
Diesel
Duzz 1020
Eddie Bauer

Erin Paige
Express
Fossil
Frette

Gap
Girlfriends
Guess?

Happy Trails
Henry Cotton's
House of Flys
ISDA & Co Outlet

J.Crew
J.Jill
Jennifer Croll/Croll Sport
Levi Strauss

Luba
Macy's
Mars Mercantile
Neiman Marcus

Nordstrom
Ocean Front Walkers
Oilily
Old Navy

Paul Frank
Piedmont
Positively Haight Street
Rolo Undercover

Saks Fifth Avenue
Scheuer Linens
Studio On Chestnut
Stüssy

Sugar Shack
Therapy
True
Twenty One

Urban Outfitters
Villains Vault
Walkershaw

Women's Classic

Bloomingdale's
Button Down
Hermès

Jaeger
Lily Samii Collection
Liz Claiborne

Macy's
Neiman Marcus
Nordstrom

Ralph Lauren
Saks Fifth Avenue
St. John

Women's Consignment

Cris
The Designer Consigner

Good Byes

Women's Contemporary

A Girl and her Dog
A Motion Studio
Ab Fits
Abigail Morgan

agnès b.
Ambiance
American Rag Cie
Annies

Anthropologie
Azadeh
Babette
The Bar

BCBG max azria
bebe
Behind the Post Office
Bettina

Bloomingdale's
Blu
Boutique Here
Brown Eyed Girl

Bryan Lee
Buu
Cara Mia
Cicada

Cielo
Coquette
Couture
Dantone

Dean Hutchinson
Dema
Designer's Club
Diana Slavin

Dish
Dreamweaver
dress
emily lee

Erica Tanov
Fife
Fitelle
French Connection

Georgiou
The Grocery Store
Haseena
Heather

Heidi Says
Henry Cotton's
hrm Boutique

jim-elle
Joanie Char
Joe Pye
Jorja

Kati Koós
Lilith
MAC
Macy's

Manifesto:
Margaret O'Leary
Martha Egan
Metier

Minnie Wilde
Mio
Mona Lisa
Neiman Marcus

Nida
Nordstrom
Oceana Rain
Ooma

Ovation
Peluche
Rabat
The Rafaels

Riki
Riley James
Rin
Rolo SoMa

Saks Fifth Avenue
Sarah Shaw
She
Sisley

Sugar Poppy
Sunhee Moon
Susan
Therapy

TSE
UKO
Valbruna
Versace Jeans Couture

Villains Vault
Wilkes Bashford
WilkesSport
Workshop

Yoya Boutique
Zeni

Women's Custom Tailoring

Azadeh
By Emily

Women's Dance & Workout Apparel

Body Options
City Fitness
1887 Dance Shoppe
GapBody

Lady Foot Locker
On the Run
Puma
See Jane Run

Women's Designer

Betsey Johnson
Bottega Veneta
Burberry
Chanel

Christian Dior
Emporio Armani
Escada

Gianni Versace
Giorgio Armani
Gucci

Hermès
Louis Vuitton
Marc Jacobs
MaxMara

Mona Lisa
Net-a-Porter
Prada

Ralph Lauren
St. John
Yves Saint Laurent

Women's Discount

Burlington Coat Factory
DSW Shoe Warehouse
Golden Bear Sportswear
Jeremys

Loehmann's
Marshalls
Rolo Garage
Ross Dress for Less

Women's Ethnic

Bombay Bazaar/Bombay Sari Palace

Women's Eveningwear & Special Occasion

Atelier des Modistes
The Bar
By Emily

Cicada
Jennifer Croll/Croll Sport
Jessica McClintock
Jin Wang

Jorja
Lily Samii Collection
Max Nugus Haute Couture

Neiman Marcus
Saks Fifth Avenue
St. John

Categories

Women's Handbags

April in Paris
Bloomingdale's
Bottega Veneta
Coach

Cole Haan
Dantone
Flight 001
Ghurka

Gucci
Hermès
Kate Spade
Kenneth Cole

Louis Vuitton
Macy's
Maison De Belles Choses
Marc Jacobs

Neiman Marcus
Nordstrom
The Sak
Saks Fifth Avenue

Salvatore Ferragamo
Therapy
Wilsons Leather
Yak Pak Store

Women's Hats

Alternative Design Studio
Mill Valley Hat Box
Mrs Dewson's Hats

Women's Hosiery

Aricie
Bloomingdale's
Macy's
Neiman Marcus

Nordstrom
Piedmont
Saks Fifth Avenue
Wolford

Women's Juniors

Bloomingdale's
Diesel
Express

Fossil
Gap

Macy's
Nordstrom
Old Navy

Urban Outfitters

Women's Leather

Fog City Leather
Golden Bear Sportswear
Knitz & Leather
Lava 9

North Beach Leather
Stormy Leather
Wilsons Leather

Women's Lingerie

Alla Prima
Aricie
Bloomingdale's

Carol Doda's Champagne &
  Lace Lingerie Boutique
Chadwicks of London

Dark Garden
GapBody
Macy's

My Boudoir
Neiman Marcus
Nordstrom

Piedmont
Romantasy Exquisite
  Corsetry

Saks Fifth Avenue
Sugarpussy
Toujours Fine Lingerie

Maternity

A Pea in the Pod
dress

Japanese Weekend
  Maternity

Mimi Maternity
Mom's the Word

Women's Petite Sizes

Bloomingdale's
Liz Claiborne

Macy's
Nordstrom

Women's Plus Sizes

Bloomingdale's
Harper Greer

Macy's
Nordstrom

Women's Secondhand

Buffalo Exchange
Crossroads Trading
  Company

Good Byes
Mars Mercantile

Women's Shirts

Bloomingdale's
fil à fil
Liz Claiborne
Macy's
Neiman Marcus

Nordstrom
Saks Fifth Avenue
Talbots
Thomas Pink
Wilkes Bashford

Stores by Category

Women's Shoes

Aerosoles
Aldo
Arthur Beren Shoes

Astrid's Rabat Shoes &
   Accessories
Birkenstock SF

Bloomingdale's
Bulo
Camper

Charles David
Coach
Cole Haan

Crosswalk Specialty Shoes
Daljeets
Dantone
DSW Shoe Warehouse

ecco
Enzo Angiolini
Fetish

Gimme Shoes
Gucci
John Fluevog Shoes
Kate Spade

Kenneth Cole
Luichiny
Macy's

Neiman Marcus
Nine West
Nordstrom

Paolo
Rabat
Rockport

Saks Fifth Avenue
Salvatore Ferragamo
Shaw Shoes

ShoeBiz
Shoesizes
Skechers USA
Smash Footwear

Steve Madden
Subterranean Shoe Room
Villains Vault

Walking Co
Wilkes Bashford
WilkesSport

Women's Swimwear

Alla Prima
Bloomingdale's
Canyon Beachwear
Macy's

Neiman Marcus
Nordstrom
Saks Fifth Avenue
Waterlilies

Women's Vintage & Retro

Aaardvarks
American Rag Cie
DEPARTURES, from the
   Past

Guys & Dolls Vintage
Held Over
La Rosa

Old Vogue
Retro Fit Vintage
Satellite Vintage
Schauplatz

Sparky's Vintage Clothing
Ver Unica
The Wasteland

Women's Young & Trendy

Arden B.
Bloomingdale's
Clobba

Coquette
Duzz 1020
Macy's

Nordstrom
Twenty One
Urban Outfitters

Weston Wear
Wet Seal
X Generation

Men's Business Apparel—European

Barcelino
BillyBlue
Bloomingdale's

Cable Car Clothiers
Courtoué
David Stephen

Fenzi Uomo
Gene Hiller
L'Uomo International

Neiman Marcus
Saks Men's Store
Uomo

Men's Business Apparel—Traditional

Alfred Dunhill
Brooks Brothers

The Hound
Saks Men's Store

Men's Cashmere/Knitwear

House of Cashmere
Margaret O'Leary
Three Bags Full

TSE
Uomo

Men's Casual

A/X Armani Exchange
Abercrombie & Fitch
All American Boy
American Eagle Outfitters

Banana Republic
Benetton
Bloomingdale's
Body Body Wear

Body/Citizen
Brooks Brothers
Button Down
Cal Surplus

City Fitness
Club Monaco
Daljeets
Diesel

Eddie Bauer
Express
Fossil
Gap

Guess?
Henry Cotton's

House of Flys
IN-JEAN-IOUS
ISDA & Co Outlet

J.Crew
Jennifer Croll/Croll Sport
Kenneth Cole
Levi Strauss

Macy's
Mars Mercantile
Neiman Marcus
Nomads

Nordstrom
Ocean Front Walkers
Old Navy
Paul Frank

Positively Haight Street
Redfive
Rolo 450
Rolo Undercover

Saks Men's Store
Stüssy
Therapy
True

Union Square N.F.L. Sports
Urban Outfitters

Villains Vault
Workwear

Men's Contemporary

A Motion Studio
Ab Fits
agnès b.
American Rag Cie

Bloomingdale's
Body Body Wear
Button Down
Citizen

Couture
French Connection
Gene Hiller
Good Byes

Henry Cotton's
hrm Boutique
Lorenzini

MAC
Neiman Marcus
The News

Nida
The Rafaels
Rolo on Market
Rolo SoMa

Saks Men's Store
Sean
She
Sisley

Smith Williams
UKO
Uomo
Valbruna

Versace Jeans Couture
Villains Vault
Wilkes Bashford

WilkesSport
Zeni

Men's Custom Tailoring

Courtoué

Men's Designer

Burberry
Emporio Armani
Gianni Versace

Giorgio Armani
Gucci
Hermès

Louis Vuitton
Marc Jacobs
MaxMara

Ralph Lauren
Yves Saint Laurent

Men's Discount

Burlington Coat Factory
DSW Shoe Warehouse
Golden Bear Sportswear
Jeremys

Loehmann's
Marshalls
The Men's Wearhouse
Ross Dress for Less

Men's Ethnic

Bombay Bazaar/Bombay
  Sari Palace

Men's Formalwear

Gingiss Formal Wear

Selix

Men's Hats

Alternative Design Studio
Cable Car Clothiers

Mill Valley Hat Box
Mrs Dewson's Hats

Men's Juniors

Bloomingdale's
Diesel

Macy's
Nordstrom

Express
Fossil
Gap

Old Navy
Urban Outfitters

Men's Leather

Fog City Leather
Golden Bear Sportswear
Lava 9
Louis Vuitton

North Beach Leather
Stormy Leather
Wilsons Leather

Men's Leathergoods, Bags & Briefcases

Bottega Veneta
Coach
Cole Haan
Flight 001

Kenneth Cole
Neiman Marcus
Saks Men's Store
Salvatore Ferragamo

Ghurka
Hermès
Kate Spade

Wilkes Bashford
Wilsons Leather
Yak Pak Store

Men's Secondhand

Buffalo Exchange
Crossroads Trading
  Company

Good Byes
Mars Mercantile

Men's Shirts

Bloomingdale's
Courtoué
Fenzi Uomo
fil à fil

Nordstrom
Saks Men's Store
Sean
Smith Williams

Kweejibo Clothing
  Company
Macy's
Neiman Marcus

Thomas Pink
Uomo
Walkershaw

Categories

Men's Shoes

The Alden Shop
Aldo
Allen Edmonds
Arthur Beren Shoes

Astrid's Rabat Shoes &
  Accessories
Birkenstock SF
Bloomingdale's

Bulo
Coach
Cole Haan
Crosswalk Specialty Shoes

Daljeets
DSW Shoe Warehouse
ecco
Gimme Shoes

Gucci
John Fluevog Shoes
Johnston & Murphy
Kenneth Cole

Luichiny
Macy's
Neiman Marcus
Nordstrom

Paolo
Rabat
Rockport
Saks Men's Store

Salvatore Ferragamo
ShoeBiz
Shoesizes
Skechers USA

Smash Footwear
Steve Madden
Subterranean Shoe Room
Villains Vault

Walking Co
Wilkes Bashford
WilkesSport

Men's Swimwear

Bloomingdale's
Canyon Beachwear
Macy's

Neiman Marcus
Nordstrom
Saks Men's Store

Men's Undergarments

Bloomingdale's
Carol Doda's Champagne &
  Lace Lingerie Boutique
GapBody
Macy's

Neiman Marcus
Nordstrom
Piedmont
Saks Men's Store

Men's Vintage & Retro

Aaardvarks
American Rag Cie
DEPARTURES, from the
  Past

Guys & Dolls Vintage
Held Over
La Rosa

Old Vogue
Retro Fit Vintage
Satellite Vintage
Schauplatz

Sparky's Vintage Clothing
Ver Unica
The Wasteland

Men's Young & Trendy

Macy's
Nordstrom

True
Urban Outfitters

Unisex Accessories

Cal Surplus
Catnip & Bones

Lost Horizon
Piedmont

Unisex Athletic

Fleet Feet Sports
Foot Locker
Harputs

MetroSport
New Balance
Niketown

Hoy's Sports
Lombardi Sports

On the Run
Puma

Unisex Department Stores

Bloomingdale's
Macy's
Neiman Marcus

Nordstrom
Saks Fifth Avenue

Unisex Jeans

Ab Fits
Bloomingdale's
House of Blue Jeans
Levi Strauss

Lucky Brand
Macy's
Nordstrom

Unisex Outdoor Sports Equipment & Apparel

Any Mountain
Don Sherwood Golf &
  Tennis World

Niketown
The North Face
On the Run

Foot Locker
Lady Foot Locker
Lombardi Sports
Marmot Mountain Works

Patagonia
Puma
REI
Valbruna

Categories

Children's Clothing

Anthropologie
Benetton
Bloomingdale's
Burberry

The Children's Place
The Disney Store
Dottie Doolittle
Eddie Bauer

Frette
Gap Kids & Baby Gap
House of Blue Jeans
Jonathan Kaye Baby

Kids Only
KinderSport
La Maison de la
    Bouquetière

Macy's
Maison De Belles Choses
Manifesto:
Minis

Mudpie
Nordstrom
Oilily
Ross Dress for Less

Small Frys
Talbots
This Little Piggy Wears
    Cotton

Thursday's Child
Tuffy's Hopscotch
Walkershaw
Yountville

Children's Shoes

The Junior Boot Shop
Skechers USA
Wavy Footprints

Health & Beauty

Barbers

Haircuts: Unisex

Haircuts: Children

Hair Salons

Hair Removal

Beauty Treatments

Manicures

Day Spas (Men & Women)

Fitness Studios

Pilates/Mat Classes

Yoga

Massage Therapists

Tanning Salons

Bridal Consultants

Make-up Artists

Barbers

Asano's Barber Shop
3312 Sacramento Street
San Francisco 94118

415-567-3335
Tues-Sat 8:30-5:30

Lombardo's Barber Shop
1508 Union Street
San Francisco 94123

415-441-0356
Tues-Sat 7:30-4

Louie's Barber Shop
422 Castro Street
San Francisco 94114

415-552-8472
Mon-Sat 9-6

The New Chicago Barbershop No. 3
1551 Fillmore Street
San Francisco 94115

415-563-9793
Tues-Thurs 9-5:30
Fri-Sat 9-6

Haircuts: Unisex

Nice Cuts
2187 Union Street
San Francisco 94123

415-929-7744
Mon-Fri 11-7:30
Sat 9-6, Sun 11-6

Nice Cuts
1508 Haight Street
San Francisco 94117

415-255-4570
Mon-Fri 10-7
Sat 9-6, Sun 11-5

Supercuts
2306 Fillmore Street
San Francisco 94115
www.supercuts.com

415-474-9652
Mon-Fri 9-8
Sat 9-7, Sun 10-6

Supercuts
18 Battery
San Francisco 94111

415-391-5340
Mon-Fri 7-7

Haircuts: Children

Peppermint Cuts
1772 Lombard Street
San Francisco 94123

415-292-6177
Mon-Sat 10-6
(by appointment only)

Snippety Crickets
3562 Sacramento Street
San Francisco 94118

415-441-9363
Daily 10-6 (Sat 9-6)

Hair Salons

Ana Walt Total Body Salon
55 Grant Avenue, 4th floor
San Francisco 94108
www.anawalt.net

415-397-9767
Tues & Sat 9-6, Wed 9:30-7
Thurs 9-8, Fri 9-7

Au Top Coiffure
305 Grant Avenue, 6th floor
San Francisco 94108

415-693-9999
Tues-Sat 9-6
www.autopsalon.com

Cinta Salon
23 Grant Avenue
San Francisco 94108

415-989-1000
Mon-Sat 9-6, (Wed-Thurs 9-8)
www.cinta.com

Cowboys & Angels
207 Powell Street, 4th floor
San Francisco 94102

415-362-8516
Tues-Wed, Fri 9-5
Thurs 11-6, Sat 9-4

diPietro Todd Salon
177 Post Street, 2nd floor
San Francisco 94108
www.dipietrotodd.com

415-397-0177
Tues-Fri 9-6
(Thurs 9-7), Sat 9-5

diPietro Todd Salon
2239 Fillmore Street
San Francisco 94115

415-674-4366
Tues-Sat 10-7

Elevation Salon & Café
451 Bush Street
San Francisco 94108

415-392-2969
Mon-Sat 9-6 (Thurs,Fri 9-7)

Glama-Rama
417 South Van Ness Avenue
San Francisco 94103

415-861-4526
Tues-Sat 10-6
www.glamarama.com

Hair Play
1599 Dolores Street
San Francisco 94110
www.hairplay.com

415-550-1656
Sun-Mon 12-6
Tues-Fri 12-8
Sat 10-6

Joseph Cozza Salon
30 Maiden Lane, 5th floor
San Francisco 94108

415-433-3030
Tues-Sat 9-6 (Thurs 9-7:30)
www.josephcozzasalon.com

Louie
4 Brady Street
San Francisco 94103

415-864-3012
Tues-Sat 10-6

77 Maiden Lane Salon & Spa
77 Maiden Lane, 2nd floor
San Francisco 94108
www.77maidenlane.com

415-391-7777
Mon, Sat 9-6
Tues-Wed, Fri 9-7
Thurs 9-8, Sun 10-6

Mister Lee
834 Jones Street
San Francisco 94109
www.misterlee.com

415-474-6002
Mon-Sat 7:30-5:30
(Thurs 7:30-8)

Novella Salon & Spa
2238 Union Street
San Francisco 94123
www.novellasalonandspa.com

415-673-1929
Tues 1:30-9, Wed-Fri 9:30-9
Sat-Sun 9-7

Oxenrose
500 Hayes Street
San Francisco 94102

415-252-9723
Mon-Fri 11-8
Sat 10-7, Sun 12-7

Space
1141 Polk Street
San Francisco 94109

415-674-1997
Tues-Sat 11-6

Zendo Urban Retreat
256 Sutter Street, 2nd floor
San Francisco 94108
www.salonzendo.com

415-788-3404
Mon, Fri 10-7
Tues-Wed 10-8
Thurs 12-9, Sat 9-6, Sun 11-7

Health & Beauty

Zip Zap 415-621-1671
245 Fillmore Street Daily 11-7
San Francisco 94117

Hair Removal

Aneu Professional Skin & Laser Center 415-440-2638
2326 Fillmore Street Tues-Sat 10-6
San Francisco 94115 www.aneuskin.com

Benefit 415-567-1173
2219 Chestnut Street Mon-Wed 10-7
San Francisco 94123 Thurs-Fri 10-7:30
www.benefitcosmetics.com Sat 9-7, Sun 10-6

Benefit 415-567-0242
2117 Fillmore Street (opening times as above)
San Francisco 94115

Cinta Salon 415-989-1000
23 Grant Avenue Mon-Sat 9-6 (Wed-Thurs 9-8)
San Francisco 94108 www.cinta.com

Elizabeth Arden Red Door Salon & Spa 415-989-4888
126 Post Street, 4th floor Sun-Mon 9-6, Tues-Wed 9-7
San Francisco 94108 Thurs-Fri 9-8, Sat 8-7
www.reddoorsalons.com

Epi Center Med Spa 415-362-4754
450 Sutter Street, #1336 Tues,Thurs 10-8, Wed 9:30-6
San Francisco 94108 Fri 10-7, Sat 9-5
www.photofacial.com

Flying Beauticians/European Skincare 415-391-8929
166 Geary Street, 9th floor Mon-Sat 9-5:30 (and later by
appointment)
San Francisco 94108 www.flyingbeauticians.com

Lana Kessel at European Skincare 415-640-7652
211 Sutter Street, 2nd floor (by appointment only)
San Francisco 94108

Lori Anderson (aesthetician) 415-863-1884
375 Potrero Avenue, #4 (by appointment only
San Francisco 94013 Mon-Wed & Sat-Sun)

Relax.now 415-504-6772
339a West Portal Avenue Tues-Fri 10-8
San Francisco 94127 Sat 9-6, Sun 10-4
also at
2241 Fillmore Street n/a at press time
San Francisco 94115 www.relaxnow.net

tru 415-399-9700
750 Kearny Street Mon-Fri 9-9 (Wed 12-9)
San Francisco 94018 Sat 9-6, Sun 11-6
www.truspa.com

Yelena Spa 415-397-2484
166 Geary Street, suite 1107 Tues-Fri 9-8, Sat 8-6
San Francisco 94108 www.yelena-spa.com

Beauty Treatments

Ana Walt Total Body Salon	**415-397-9767**
55 Grant Avenue, 4th floor	Tues & Sat 9-6, Wed 9:30-7
San Francisco 94108	Thurs 9-8, Fri 9-7
www.anawalt.net

Aneu Professional Skin & Laser Center	**415-440-2638**
2326 Fillmore Street	Tues-Sat 10-6
San Francisco 94115	www.aneuskin.com

The Art of Aesthetics	**415-487-9217**
211 Church Street, suite C	Tues-Fri 11-6, Sat 10-6
San Francisco 94114	www.artofaesthetics.com

Beate Comment	**415-393-1490**
450 Sutter Street, suite 2304	Tues-Sat 9-6
San Francisco 94108

Cinta Salon	**415-989-1000**
23 Grant Avenue	Mon-Sat 9-6
San Francisco 94108	(Wed-Thurs 9-8)
www.cinta.com

Elizabeth Arden Red Door Salon & Spa	**415-989-4888**
126 Post Street, 4th floor	Sun-Mon 9-6, Tues-Wed 9-7
San Francisco 94108	Thurs-Fri 9-8, Sat 8-7
www.reddoorsalons.com

Eva Patel of the Skin Rejuvenation Clinic	**415-788-SKIN**
251 Post Street, suite 310	Tues 10-6, Wed 11-7
San Francisco 94108	every other Sat 10-4
www.skinrx.com	1st Thurs of every month 11-7

Le Sanctuaire (Rebecca Whitworth)	**415-401-6930**
(Tues-Sat and some Sundays, by appointment only)
www.lesanctuaire.com

Lisa Bradbury Skincare Salon	**415-441-7470**
1756 Fillmore Street	Mon-Tues & Fri-Sat 10-5
San Francisco 94115	(Wed-Thurs by appointment only)

Lori Anderson (aesthetician)	**415-863-1884**
375 Potrero Avenue, #4	(Mon-Wed & Sat-Sun
San Francisco 94013	by appointment only)

Marilyn Jaeger Skincare Studio	**415-751-0647**
415 Spruce Street	Mon 12-9, Wed-Thurs 8:30-9:30
San Francisco 94118	Fri 9-6, Sat 9:30-6, Sun 10-6
www.marilynjaegerskincare.com

Mary Garnett Aesthetics	**415-749-1455**
2660 Gough Street, suite 204	(by appointment only)
San Francisco 94123

Relax.now	**415-504-6772**
339-A West Portal Avenue	Tues-Fri 10-8
San Francisco 94127	Sat 9-6, Sun 10-4
also at
2241 Fillmore Street	n/a at press time
San Francisco 94115	www.relaxnow.net

Health & Beauty

Scott Fisher at
77 Maiden Lane Salon & Spa
77 Maiden Lane, 2nd floor
San Francisco 94108
www.77maidenlane.com

415-391-7777
Mon, Sat 9-6
Tues-Wed, Fri 9-7
Thurs 9-8, Sun 10-6

tru
750 Kearny Street
San Francisco 94018
www.truspa.com

415-399-9700
Mon-Fri 9-9 (Wed 12-9)
Sat 9-6, Sun 11-6

Yelena Spa
166 Geary Street, suite 1107
San Francisco 94108

415-397-2484
Tues-Fri 9-8, Sat 8-6
www.yelena-spa.com

Manicures

Dynasty Nails
107 Stevenson Street
San Francisco 94105

415-975-8654
Mon-Sat 9:30-7:30

Marilyn Jaeger Skincare Studio
415 Spruce Street
San Francisco 94118
www.marilynjaegerskincare.com

415-751-0647
Mon 12-9, Wed-Thurs 8:30-9:30
Fri 9-6, Sat 9:30-6, Sun 10-6

Nail Care For You
1507 Grant Avenue
San Francisco 94133

415-362-3347
Tues-Sat 9:30-7, Sun 10-6

Nail Pretty
3315 Sacramento Street
San Francisco 94118

415-673-9818
Mon-Fri 9:30-7:30
Sat-Sun 9-7

Relax.now
339a West Portal Avenue
San Francisco 94127
also at
2241 Fillmore Street
San Francisco 94115

415-504-6772
Tues-Fri 10-8
Sat 9-6, Sun 10-4

n/a at press time

77 Maiden Lane Salon & Spa
77 Maiden Lane, 2nd floor
San Francisco 94108
www.77maidenlane.com

415-391-7777
Mon, Sat 9-6
Tues-Wed, Fri 9-7
Thurs 9-8, Sun 10-6

Shannon Wiggins @ Beate Comment
450 Sutter Street, suite 2304
San Francisco 94108

415-393-1490
Tues-Sat 9-6

Silk Nail Salon
1425 Franklin Street
San Francisco 94109

415-885-3277
Mon-Fri 9:30-7:30
Sat 10-6, Sun 11-6

Stellar Spa
26 Tamalpais Drive
Corte Madera 94925

415-924-7300
Tues-Fri 10-8, Sat-Sun 10-6
www.stellarspa.com

tru
750 Kearny Street
San Francisco 94018
www.truspa.com

415-399-9700
Mon-Fri 9-9 (Wed 12-9)
Sat 9-6, Sun 11-6

Yelena Spa
166 Geary Street, suite 1107
San Francisco 94108

415-397-2484
Tues-Fri 9-8, Sat 8-6
www.yelena-spa.com

Day Spas (Men & Women)

The Claremont Resort & Spa
41 Tunnel Road
Berkeley 94705
www.claremontresort.com

510-549-8566
Sun-Thurs 9-7
Fri-Sat 8-9

Kabuki Springs & Spa
1750 Geary Boulevard
San Francisco 94115

415-922-6000
Daily 10-9:45
www.kabukisprings.com

Labelle Day Spas
233 Grant Avenue
San Francisco 94108
www.labelledayspas.com

415-433-7644
Mon-Fri 9-8
Sat 9-6, Sun 10-5

Labelle Day Spas
95 Town & Country Village
Palo Alto 94301

650-327-6964
Mon-Fri 8-8
Sat 8-6

Labelle Day Spas
36 Stanford Shopping Center
Palo Alto 94304

650-326-8522
Mon-Fri 8-9
Sat 8-7, Sun 10-6

Nob Hill Spa
1075 California Street
San Francisco 94108

415-345-2888
Daily 8-8
www.huntingtonhotel.com

Novella Salon & Spa
2238 Union Street
San Francisco 94123
www.novellasalon.citysearch.com

415-673-1929
Tues 1:30-9, Wed-Fri 9:30-9
Sat-Sun 9-7

Preston Wynne Spa
14567 Big Basin Way
Saratoga 95070

408-741-5525
Mon-Fri 9-9, Sat-Sun 9-5
www.prestonwynnespa.com

Re:Fresh, A Day Spa
1130 Post Street   Mon 12-8, Tues-Wed 10-8, Thurs-Sun 9-8
San Francisco 94109

415-563-2316
www.refreshdayspa.com

Relax.now
339a West Portal Avenue
San Francisco 94127
also at
2241 Fillmore Street
San Francisco 94115

415-504-6772
Tues-Fri 10-8
Sat 9-6, Sun 10-4

n/a at press time
www.relaxnow.net

Spa Nordstrom
San Francisco Shopping Centre
865 Market Street, 5th floor
San Francisco 94103   www.nordstrom.com/spanordstrom

415-977-5102
Mon-Sat 9:30-7:30
Sun 10:45-5

Spa Radiance
3011 Fillmore Street
San Francisco 94123
www.sparadiance.com

415-346-6281
Mon 10-6, Wed-Fri 9-9
Tues, Sat-Sun 9-7

Health & Beauty

Spa Seven 415-775-6546
2358 Pine Street Tues-Sun 10-7
San Francisco 94125

Stellar Spa 415-924-7300
26 Tamalpais Drive Tues-Fri 10-8, Sat-Sun 10-6
Corte Madera 94925 www.stellarspa.com

Tea Garden Springs 415-389-7123
38 Miller Avenue Daily 9:30-7:30 (Sun 10:30-7:30)
Mill Valley 94941 www.teagardensprings.com

tru 415-399-9700
750 Kearny Street Mon-Fri 9-9 (Wed 12-9)
San Francisco 94018 Sat 9-6, Sun 11-6
www.truspa.com

Yelena Spa for Women & Men 415-397-2484
166 Geary Street, suite 1107 Tues-Fri 9-8, Sat 8-6
San Francisco 94108 www.yelena-spa.com

Zendo Urban Retreat 415-788-3404
256 Sutter Street Mon, Fri 10-7, Tues-Wed 10-8
San Francisco 94108 Thurs 12-9, Sat 9-6, Sun 11-7
www.salonzendo.com

Fitness Studios

Crunch Fitness 415-931-1100
1000 Van Ness Avenue Mon-Thurs 5:30-11
San Francisco 94109 Fri 5:30-9:30, Sat-Sun 8-8
www.crunch.com

Gorilla Sports 415-474-2699
2450 Sutter Street Mon-Thurs 6-9, Fri 6-6:30
San Francisco 94115 Sat 8-5, Sun 8-11
www.gorillasports.com

Gorilla Sports 415-292-8470
2324 Chestnut Street Mon-Thurs 5:30-10
San Francisco 94123 Fri 5:30-8, Sat-Sun 7-7

Mission Cliffs Rock Climbing Center 415-550-0515
2295 Harrison Street Mon, Wed, Fri 6:30-10
San Francisco 94110 Tues,Thurs 6:30-11, Sat-Sun 10-6
www.mission-cliffs.com

Mojo Fitness/Yoga Studio 415-380-9629
8 & 16 Madrona Street Mon-Fri 7-8
Mill Valley 94941 Sat 8-1

San Francisco Bay Club 415-433-2200
150 Greenwich Street Mon-Fri 5-11
San Francisco 94111 Sat-Sun 6-9
www.sfbayclub.com

San Francisco Bay Club 415-362-7800
555 California Street Mon-Thurs 5-9:30
San Francisco 94104 Fri 5-8:30, Sat 8:30-6

Pilates/Mat Classes

A Body of Work
569 Ruger Street
San Francisco 94129

415-561-3991
Mon-Fri 7-8, Sat 8-1
www.abodyofwork-sf.com

The Body Gallery
1527 Baker Street
San Francisco 94115

415-776-6641
(by appointment only)
www.thebodygallery.com

Body Kinetics
2399 Greenwich Street
San Francisco 94123

415-931-9922
Mon-Thurs 6-9
Fri 6-8, Sat-Sun 8-6

Defy Gravity
3611 Sacramento Street, suite A
San Francisco 94118

415-409-3339
(by appointment only)
www.defygravitypilates.net

The Ellie Herman Studios
3435 Cesar Chavez Street
San Francisco 94110

415-285-5808
Daily 7-9
www.ellie.net

The Mindful Body
2876 California Street
San Francisco 94115

415-931-2639
Mon-Fri 9-9, Sat-Sun 9-7
www.themindfulbody.com

Simply Balanced
2845 California Street
San Francisco 94115

415-567-4349
(call for schedule)
www.simplybalanced.com

Yoga

Bikram's Yoga College of India
910 Columbus Avenue
San Francisco 94133

415-346-5400
(call for schedule)
www.bikramyoga.com

Bikram's Yoga College of India
1816 Magnolia Avenue
Burlingame 94010

650-552-9642
(call for schedule)

It's Yoga
848 Folsom Street
San Francisco 94107

415-543-1970
(call for schedule)
www.itsyoga.net

The Mindful Body
2876 California Street
San Francisco 94115

415-931-2639
Mon-Fri 9-9, Sat-Sun 9-7
www.themindfulbody.com

San Francisco Yoga Studio
2159 Filbert Street
San Francisco 94123

415-931-YOGA
(call for schedule)
www.usyoga.org

7th Heaven Body Awareness Center
2820 7th Street
Berkeley 94710

510-665-4300
(call for schedule)
www.7thheavenyoga.com

Spa Seven
2358 Pine Street
San Francisco 94125

415-775-6546
Tues-Sun 10-7

The Yoga Studio
650 East Blithedale Avenue
Mill Valley 94941

415-380-8800
(call for schedule)
www.yogastudiomillvalley.com

Yoga Tree
780 Stanyan Street
San Francisco 94117

415-387-4707
(call for schedule)
www.yogatreesf.com

Massage Therapists

Aquatic Massage & Bodywork Center
2366 Pine Street
San Francisco 94115

415-922-4283
(by appointment only)

Club One
535 Mason Street
San Francisco 94102

415-337-1010
Mon-Fri 5:30-10, Sat-Sun 7-7

The Mindful Body
2876 California Street
San Francisco 94115

415-931-2639
Mon-Fri 9-9, Sat-Sun 9-7
www.themindfulbody.com

Therapeia
1801 Bush Street
San Francisco 94109

415-885-4450
Mon-Fri 9-9, Sat-Sun 9-8
www.etherapeia.com

Tanning Salons

Brownie's European Tanning
1735b Union Street
San Francisco 94123

415-775-3815
Mon-Fri 8-8:30, Sat-Sun 8-7:30

Relax.now
339a West Portal Avenue
San Francisco 94127
also at
2241 Fillmore Street
San Francisco 94115

415-504-6772
Tues-Fri 10-8
Sat 9-6, Sun 10-4

n/a at press time
www.relaxnow.net

Solar Planet
3151 Fillmore Street
San Francisco 94123

415-922-7200
Mon-Fri 7-9, Sat-Sun 8-9
www.solarplanet.com

Sundays Tanning
2286 Union Street
San Francisco 94123

415-292-4490
Mon-Sat 8-10, Sun 10-6

Bridal Consultants

Connie Kearns with Bridal Network   **415-362-0199**

Laurie Arons Special Events   **415-332-0600**

Make-up Artists

Jim Avila   **415-861-2857**

Erin Gallagher   **415-819-1123**

Aida's Custom Cosmetics
1146 Chestnut Lane
Menlo Park 94025

650-327-9882
Tues-Fri 10:30-5, Sat 11-4

MAC
1833 Union Street
San Francisco 94123

415-771-6113
Mon-Sat 11-7, Sun 11-6
www.maccosmetics.com

Repairs & Services

Personal Shoppers

Dry Cleaners

Mending, Alterations, Custom Tailors

Shoe Repair

Leather Repair (Handbags &Luggage)

Trimmings (Ribbons, Buttons, etc.)

Thrift Shops

Personal Shoppers

Macy's Union Square   **415-397-3333**
170 O'Farrell Street   Mon-Sat 10-6
San Francisco 94102   Sun 11-6

Neiman Marcus   **415-362-3900**
150 Stockton Street   Mon-Sat 10-6
San Francisco 94108

Nordstrom   **415-243-8500**
865 Market Street   Mon-Sat 9:30-9, Sun 10-7
San Francisco 94103

Saks Fifth Avenue   **415-986-1958**
384 Post Street   Mon-Sat 10-6
San Francisco 94108   (and by appointment)

Dry Cleaners: Haute Couture & Bridal

DLS Clean Express   **415-333-1509**
6115 Mission Street   Mon-Sat 8:30-6:30
Daly City 94014

Lacrouts-Lyonnaise   **415-647-1534**
3359 26th Street   Mon-Fri 7-5, Sat 9-2
San Francisco 94110

Locust Cleaners   **415-346-9271**
3585 Sacramento Street   Mon-Fri 7:30-6, Sat 8:30-5
San Francisco 94118

Marina Cleaners   **415-931-3444**
3717 Buchanan Street   Mon-Thurs 6:30-8
San Francisco 94123   Fri 6:30-7, Sat 9-5

Peninou   **415-751-7050**
3707 Sacramento Street   Mon-Fri 7-6:30, Sat 9-5
San Francisco 94118   www.peninou.com

Peninou   **415-351-2554**
3063 Laguna Street   (opening times as above)
San Francisco   94123

Peninou   **650-322-7562**
558 Oak Grove Avenue   (opening times as above)
Menlo Park 94025

Dry Cleaners: Leather & Suede

Castro Village Cleaners   **415-863-1665**
4107 19th Street   Mon-Fri 7-7
San Francisco 94114   Sat 8-5, Sun 11-5

Leather Care Cleaners   **415-647-2345**
2345 Mission Street   Mon-Fri 7:30-5:30, Sat 9-5
San Francisco 94110

Wendel Leather   **415-474-4104**
1623 Polk Street   Tues-Fri 11-5, Sat 1-5
San Francisco 94109

Dry Cleaners: All-purpose

G.F.Thomas   **415-861-0969**
859 14th Street   Mon-Fri 7:30-6, Sat 7:30-1
San Francisco 94114

Mack's Valet Cleaners   **415-474-3090**
766 Post Street   Mon-Fri 7:30-7, Sat 8:30-7
San Francisco 94109

Ray's French Cleaners   **415-885-4171**
1205 Union Street   Mon-Fri 7:30-6:30, Sat 8-5
San Francisco 94109

Vogue Cleaners   **415-388-5547**
950 Redwood Highway   Mon-Fri 7-6:30, Sat 9-5
Mill Valley 94941

Vogue Cleaners   **415-388-3035**
77 Miller Avenue   Mon-Fri 7-6, Sat 9-5
Mill Valley 94941

Mending, Alterations, Custom Design Tailors

By Emily   **415-440-0081**
2271 Union Street   Tues-Sat 12-6
San Francisco 94123

Cable Car Tailors   **415-781-4636**
200 O'Farrell Street   Mon-Sat 8-6
San Francisco 94104

Castro Street Tailors   **415-431-7222**
550 Castro Street, #A   Mon-Fri 8-6, Sat 9-5
San Francisco 94104

Escobar Brothers   **415-986-3386**
391 Sutter Street   Mon-Fri 9-6, Sat 10-5
San Francisco 94108

Locust Cleaners   **415-346-9271**
3585 Sacramento Street   Mon-Fri 7:30-6, Sat 8:30-5
San Francisco 94118

Peter Panos   **415-986-8487**
109 Geary Street, floor M   Mon-Fri 10:30-6
San Francisco 94108   Sat 10:30-5

Suzanne George Shoes (custom shoes)   **415-775-1775**
Noe Valley Workshop   Mon-Fri 8-4, Sat 8-2 (and by
San Francisco 94131   appointment)

Shoe Repair

Anthony's Shoe Repair   **415-781-1338**
30 Geary Street   Mon-Fri 8-5:30, Sat 9-5
San Francisco 94108   www.shoerepair.com

Galletti Bros   **415-982-2897**
427 Columbus Avenue   Mon-Fri 8-6, Sat 9-6
San Francisco 94133

Tony's Shoe Repair   **415-388-5935**
38 Corte Madera Avenue   Mon-Fri 9-6, Sat 9-4
Mill Valley 94941

Leather Repair (Handbags & Luggage)

Main Luggage Repair   **415-673-2286**
1425 Bush Street   Mon-Fri 8-5, Sat 10-3
San Francisco 94108

Trimmings (Ribbons, Buttons, Feathers, Fabric and Odds & Ends)

Bell'occhio   **415-864-4048**
8 Brady Street   Tues-Sat 11-5
San Francisco 94103   www.bellocchio.com

Britex Fabrics   **415-392-2910**
146 Geary Street   Mon-Sat 9:30-6 (Thurs-Fri 9:30-7)
San Francisco 94108   www.britexfabrics.com

Buttons & Bows   **415-453-5080**
237 San Anselmo Avenue   Tues-Sat 10-5:30
San Anselmo 94960

Lacis   **510-843-7290**
2982 Adeline Street   Mon-Fri 1-5:30, Sat 11-5:30
Berkeley 94703   (for vintage lace and trim)
www.lacis.com

Mendel's Far Out Fabrics   **415-621-1287**
1556 Haight Street   Mon-Fri 10-5:50
San Francisco 94117   Sat 10-5:20, Sun 12-4:50
www.mendels.com
(selection of fabric, ribbons, buttons and trim)

The Ribbonerie   **415-626-6184**
191 Potrero Avenue   Tues-Fri 11-6, Sat 11-5
San Francisco 94103   www.theribbonerie.com

Tail of the Yak   **510-841-9891**
2632 Ashby Avenue   Mon-Sat 11-5:30
Berkeley 94705

Satin Moon Fabrics   **415-668-1623**
32 Clement Street   Tues-Sat 11:40-6 (Thurs 11:40-7)
San Francisco 94118

Thrift Shops

Next To New Shop   **415-567-1627**
2226 Fillmore Street   Mon-Sat 10-5:30
San Francisco 94115   Sun 12-4

Seconds To Go   **415-563-7806**
2252 Fillmore Street   Mon-Sat 10-5:15, Sun 1-5
San Francisco 94115

Clothes Closet   **415-929-8019**
3325 Sacramento Street   Mon-Fri 10-6, Sat 10-5
San Francisco 94118

Fashion Speak

Avant-garde: forward-thinking or advanced. When referring to art or costume, sometimes implies erotic or startling. Derived from the French for "advance guard".

Bridge collection: a collection that is priced between designer and mass market.

Couture: French word used throughout fashion industry to describe the original styles, the ultimate in fine sewing and tailoring, made of expensive fabrics, by designers. The designs are shown in collections twice a year—spring/summer and fall/winter.

Custom-made/tailor-made, also called bespoke: garments made by tailor or couture house for an individual customer following couturier's original design. Done by either fitting a model form adjusted to the customer's measurements or by several personal fittings.

Diffusion line: a designer's second and less expensive collection.

Ensemble: an entire costume, including accessories, worn at one time. Two or more items of clothing designed and coordinated to be worn together.

Fashion trend: direction in which styles, colors and fabrics are moving. Trends may be influenced by political events, films, personalities, dramas, social and sporting events or indeed any human activity.

Faux: false or counterfeit, imitation: used in connection with gems, pearls and leathers. Faux fur (fake fur) is commonplace today, as is what is sometimes known as "pleather" (plastic leather). Artificial gems, especially pearls, are often made from a fine kind of glass known as "paste", and are accordingly sometimes called "paste" for short.

Haberdashery: a store that sells men's apparel and furnishings.

Knock-off: trade term for the copying of an item of apparel, e.g. a dress or a coat, in a lower price line. Similar to piracy.

Made-to-measure: clothing (dress, suit, shirt etc) made according to individual's measurement. No fittings required.

One-off: a unique, one-of-a-kind item that will not be found in any other store or produced again in the future, e.g. a customized denim skirt or a rare vintage cocktail dress. Can also refer to made-to-measure and couture garments designed for a particular person and/or event, such as a dress for the Oscars.

Prêt-à-porter: French term which literally means ready-to-wear, i.e. to take (or wear) straight out of the shop.

Ready-to-wear (rtw): apparel that is mass-produced in standard sizes. Records of the ready-to-wear industry tabulated in the U.S. Census of 1860 included hoop skirts, cloaks, and mantillas; from 1890 shirtwaists and wrappers were added; and, after 1930, dresses.

5 very good reasons why you should become a *Where to Wear* online subscriber

1. Access the guide online from wherever you are.

2. Take the guide on a laptop or CD ROM.

3. Find a particular designer, type of clothing or boutique easily by just typing in what you want and seeing the result.

4. Results printed out to show information and location, member concessions, special offers and promotions from stores.

5. Exclusive seasonal offers available to *Where to Wear* members only from selected stores.

Visit our new exclusive members website at

www.wheretowear.com/member.htm

How to order *Where to Wear*

Where to Wear publishes guides to the following cities: *London*, *New York*, *Paris*, *Los Angeles*, *San Francisco* and *Italy* (which includes Florence, Milan and Rome). Each edition retails at £9.99 or $12.95.

There is also a gift box set, *Shopping Guides to the World's Fashion Capitals*, available for £29.99 or $49.99 which includes the **London**, **New York**, **Paris** and *Italy (Milan, Florence, and Rome)* guides (four books for the price of three).

If you live in the UK or Europe, you can order your copies of *Where to Wear* by contacting our London office at:

10 Cinnamon Row
Plantation Wharf
London SW11 3TW
TEL: 020 7801 1381
EMAIL: wheretowear@onetel.net.uk

If you live in the USA, you can order your copies of *Where to Wear* by contacting our New York office at:

666 Fifth Avenue
PMB 377
New York, NY 10103
TEL: 212-969-0138
TOLL-FREE: 1-877-714-SHOP (7467)
EMAIL: wheretowear@aol.com

Or simply log on to our website: www.wheretowear.com
Where to Wear delivers worldwide.

Notes

Notes